in defense of Easter

Answering Critical Challenges
to the Resurrection of Jesus

tim chaffey

Printed in the United States of America.

First Printing, 2014
Second Printing, 2016

ISBN 978-0-9960087-0-9

Midwest Apologetics
www.midwestapologetics.org

Portions of chapters 1–10, 12–17 and 24 consist of articles written
by Tim Chaffey for Answers in Genesis, the copyright owner of
such articles, and are included by licensed permission of Answers
in Genesis. For more information regarding Answers in Genesis,
go to www.AnswersinGenesis.org, or www.CreationMuseum.org,
or www.ArkEncounter.com.

Unless otherwise stated all Scripture taken from the New King
James Version®. Copyright © 1982 by Thomas Nelson, Inc.
Used by permission. All rights reserved.

Praise for In Defense of Easter

"Challenges to Jesus' Resurrection are frequently made on the popular level, and answers must be forthcoming. Tim Chaffey's volume responds to many of these contemporary questions, as well as moving beyond arguments and evidences to the application of Resurrection truth. What difference can belief in the Resurrection mean for believers today? This volume is an accessible handbook that covers a wide range of issues, both theoretical as well as practical. I very much enjoyed my time with it and recommend it to those who love this topic and are interested in material that is not readily available elsewhere."

—Gary R. Habermas, *Distinguished Research Professor, Liberty University & Theological Seminary*

"Tim Chaffey has done his homework for this book. He has paid careful attention to the details of all the relevant biblical texts regarding the Resurrection of Jesus, and he is thoroughly informed on the multitude of arguments and objections raised by skeptics who have attempted to explain away the empty tomb. His tone is respectful but clear and firm as he dismantles the fallacious reasoning of the enemies of the gospel. Unlike many books on the subject, Tim draws out the connection between the Resurrection and the literal history in Genesis 1–11. I also really appreciated the way he ended the book by sharing how the reality of the Resurrection of Jesus impacted his own life in a time of great testing and by his separate challenge to both his Christian and non-Christian readers. Every Christian will profit by reading this excellent defense of the Resurrection and the gospel. Nonbelievers will be challenged to carefully consider the Messiah Jesus who died for their sins and rose from the dead to restore them to a right relationship with their Creator, if they will simply turn from their sin and trust in Him as Lord and Savior. I heartily recommend this book!"

—Terry Mortenson, *Ph.D., Coventry University (UK); Speaker and Researcher, Answers in Genesis*

For my wonderful parents. Thank you for teaching me from my early years to love and serve our risen Savior.

Table of Contents

Section Three: Other Relevant Questions

Acknowledgments

Throughout my life, countless people have played a role in helping me understand the Resurrection with greater clarity. To each of you, I offer a sincere "Thank you!"

Others have played a more direct role in this book's coming to fruition and deserve special mention and thanks: Steve Golden (editing, interior layout), Benjamin Iocco (cover art), James de Leon (cover layout), Terry Mortenson and Roger Patterson (content review), and Abigail Westbrook (advertisement design).

I also want to thank Dr. Gary Habermas for your tireless study and promotion of the Resurrection. I was blessed to study under you for two courses where this topic was discussed at length, and God used your efforts to develop in me a greater love for this tremendous miracle.

Thank you to my family for granting me the many hours tucked away downstairs to write. An extra special thanks goes to my wife for putting up with me through all the long discussions and rewrites, and also for your suggestions and everything else that goes into completing a book.

Finally, and most importantly, I thank my Lord and Savior Jesus Christ. Thank You for bearing my sins on the Cross and for demonstrating your power over death that first Easter morning. Jesus, I pray that this book will magnify Your name and point others to You.

Preface

Good books on the Resurrection of Jesus Christ are not rare.
I have at least a dozen on my shelf and have read even more
while researching for this volume. Some are massive academic
treatments of the topic, explaining the nuances of the original
languages and diving deeper than many would ever imagine.
Others are more devotionally oriented, emphasizing the practical
aspects of the Lord's conquering of death. Still other texts focus
primarily on apologetic matters, defending this vital doctrine
from skeptical and critical attacks. So why is this book needed?
How does it differ from the rest?

In Defense of Easter blends qualities from each of these
approaches. There is a strong apologetic emphasis throughout
this work. Christians should be prepared to give a defense for
their beliefs (1 Peter 3:15) and need to realize that, in addition to
the infallible biblical proclamation of the event, the Resurrection
of Jesus stands on solid historical ground. Hundreds of people
saw Jesus alive after His death by Crucifixion, and many reliable
eyewitnesses wrote about their experiences with the risen Lord.
The central teaching of Christianity is utterly defensible and must
be proclaimed as such.

This book interacts with the leading scholarship on the
subject today. But instead of keeping the content at the academic
level comprehensible only to those with extensive training, I have
endeavored to make this research accessible to the average reader,
even those unfamiliar with the topic. Everyone needs to know
these fundamental truths. Documentation provided in footnotes

directs interested readers to resources that can help them dive deeper into the many issues addressed.

At the same time, this work underscores the enormously practical elements of Christ's Resurrection and frequently highlights the gospel message. The fact that God raised Jesus from the dead is a source of comfort and hope for believers as it secured our eternal life and assures us that we will see our believing loved ones again. Since Jesus is alive and at the Father's right hand, He stands up for us, interceding on our behalf when Satan, the accuser, lays charges against us. Furthermore, the Resurrection of Jesus serves as proof that His message was true, that our faith is not in vain, and that He will one day raise us to live eternally with Him.

While blending these features of other books on the subject, *In Defense of Easter* differs in some respects. Many of the apologetic works dealing with the Resurrection have a broader focus. They spend a great deal of space addressing the reliability of the New Testament, the possibility of miracles, and an assortment of other issues. These topics are important, and I would urge readers to study them, but I do not want to detract in any way from the Resurrection. The following chapters are designed to zero in on critical questions about that glorious miracle in a tomb outside of Jerusalem nearly two millennia ago.

Prepare yourself for a journey to the dawn of the Christian faith and get ready to acquire a deeper appreciation for the risen Lord and Savior.

Section One:
The Case for the Resurrection

1 Why Is the Resurrection of Jesus Christ Important?

I enthusiastically look forward to Easter each year since I often have opportunities to speak on the most exciting topic—the Resurrection of Jesus Christ. I also love singing the classic hymns about the Crucifixion and Resurrection. Of course, I enjoy writing and speaking about creation, evolution, Genesis, the age of the earth, biblical authority, and the biblical worldview. Still, no topic thrills me as much as thinking about that glorious Sunday morning when an angel rolled the stone away and the death-conquering Savior exited the tomb that had housed His dead body for a short while—since this miracle secured the hope of our salvation.

In Their Sandals

I try to think about what it must have been like to be in the disciples' sandals when they saw the risen Savior for the first time. Imagine having all your hopes and dreams dashed to pieces as the person you put your faith in was mercilessly beaten and then brutally executed upon the Cross. The agony and despair felt by the disciples during that time is nearly impossible to fathom. They had left everything for Jesus, and now He was gone, leaving the disciples to wallow in their sorrow, confusion, and shame for following a pretender Messiah who was now viewed as someone accursed by God (Isaiah 53:4; Galatians 3:13).

Picture yourself in Peter's position. The brash and outspoken disciple who said he would die for his Lord was suffering the depths of despondency, having cowardly rejected Jesus multiple times. Suddenly, Mary Magdalene shows up and says that the body of Christ is missing and none of the women who went to the tomb that morning know where it is (John 20:2). Did a flash of hope pierce Peter's mind at that moment? Did anger flow through him as he pondered even more embarrassment at the thought of the Lord's body being dishonorably treated? What did he think when he entered the tomb and saw the linen cloths lying where Christ's body had recently been? Did he plunge deeper into misery as he walked away that morning (John 20:10)?

Peter's utter hopelessness was finally shattered later that day when Jesus appeared to him alive and well (Luke 24:34; 1 Corinthians 15:5). But this was no fluke appearance—it was not a vision or hallucination. Jesus had already appeared to Mary Magdalene (John 20:11–18), and later that day to two disciples on the road to Emmaus (Luke 24:15), and then to the whole group of disciples minus Thomas (Luke 24:36). Over the next several weeks, Jesus showed Himself alive by "many infallible proofs" to the disciples (Acts 1:3), and on one occasion He appeared to over 500 people at once (1 Corinthians 15:6).

A short while later, the disciples, filled by the Holy Spirit and the knowledge of the risen Savior, went forth in absolute confidence that their message was true and turned the world upside down with the gospel, unwaveringly facing persecution and death along the way.

The Importance of the Resurrection

At the heart of their message was the Resurrection. Peter's sermon on the Day of Pentecost centered on Jesus rising from the dead (Acts 2:24–36). Paul focused on the event as well. Some of the philosophers in Athens thought he was strange because he preached about Jesus and the Resurrection (Acts 17:18). When given an opportunity to speak at the Areopagus, Paul delivered his message and then said that God had given "assurance of this to all by raising [Jesus] from the dead" (Acts 17:31). In fact, Acts covers 12 major addresses as the gospel message spread from Jerusalem to the rest of the Roman Empire, and according to Merrill C. Tenney, "In each stage of presentation the place of the resurrection is constant; it is never deprecated or ignored but occupies a prominent place."[1]

Sadly, it seems that this event no longer enjoys a prominent place for many Christians, often being relegated to the topic of the sermon only on Easter Sunday. And I've been to churches where it doesn't even get that much attention. Some focus so much on the Crucifixion and what Jesus accomplished there that the Resurrection is treated like an afterthought. I call this the Passion Syndrome, so named for the formula followed in Mel Gibson's film, *The Passion of the Christ*. The movie spent most of its two-plus hours illustrating the horrors of Christ's torture and death, but just over one minute on Jesus rising from the dead at the end of the film. See chapter 23 for reasons why the Resurrection is often overlooked.

Please don't misunderstand me. The Crucifixion is absolutely essential, and we must never shy away from discussing the Cross, but the Resurrection is the flip-side of that coin. Without the Resurrection, Christ's death would be the end of our hopes, and of course, without the Crucifixion, Jesus could not have risen from the dead. Both are necessary for the forgiveness of sins (Ephesians 1:7; 1 Corinthians 15:17).[2] In fact, Paul told the Corinthians that the gospel he preached was "that Christ died for our sins according to the Scriptures, and that He was buried, and that He rose again the third day according to the Scriptures," and that He was seen by numerous people (1 Corinthians 15:1–8).

---

[1] Merrill C. Tenney, *The Reality of the Resurrection* (Chicago, IL: Moody Press, 1972), n.p. Electronic version of the chapter in which this statement appears is available from <www.rediscoveringthebible.com/Realitych3.pdf>. Accessed February 1, 2013.

[2] Mathewson wrote, "[I]n 1 Corinthians 15:17 Paul makes it clear that we are still in our sins if Christ has not been raised. So while the death and resurrection of Jesus Christ were separate events, they are inseparable elements when it comes to providing forgiveness for our sins." Steven Mathewson, *Risen: 50 Reasons Why the Resurrection Changed Everything* (Grand Rapids, MI: Baker Books, 2013), p. 23.

For the past few years as I have read through the New Testament, I have paid special attention to the Resurrection and have been amazed at just how frequently the writers mention the topic. Paul devoted an entire chapter to the subject and discussed its significance to the Christian faith.

> And if Christ is not risen, then our preaching is empty and your faith is also empty. Yes, and we are found false witnesses of God, because we have testified of God that He raised up Christ, whom He did not raise up—if in fact the dead do not rise. For if the dead do not rise, then Christ is not risen. And if Christ is not risen, your faith is futile; you are still in your sins! Then also those who have fallen asleep in Christ have perished. If in this life only we have hope in Christ, we are of all men the most pitiable. (1 Corinthians 15:14–19)

If Jesus did not rise from the dead, then Christianity would be a false religion, we would have no hope, our loved ones would be gone for good, and we would still be in our sins. I appreciate Philip Schaff's summary on the importance of the Resurrection based on Paul's words.

> The Christian church rests on the resurrection of its Founder. Without this fact the church could never have been born, or if born, it would soon have died a natural death. The miracle of the resurrection and the existence of Christianity are so closely connected that they must stand or fall together. If Christ was raised from the dead, then all his other miracles are sure, and our faith is impregnable; if he was not raised, he died in vain and our faith is vain. It was only his resurrection that made his death available for our atonement, justification and salvation; without the resurrection, his death would be the grave of our hopes; we should be still unredeemed and under the power of our sins. A gospel of a dead Saviour would be a contradiction and wretched delusion. This is the reasoning of St. Paul, and its force is irresistible.

The resurrection of Christ is therefore emphatically a test question upon which depends the truth or falsehood of the Christian religion. It is either the greatest miracle or the greatest delusion which history records.[3]

Now consider the alternative. If Jesus actually rose from the dead, then an astonishing miracle was performed and through this act God placed His seal of approval on the life and work of Jesus for all to see.[4] In other words, the Resurrection shows us that God affirmed the truth of Christ's teachings, meaning that Jesus is exactly who He claimed to be—the eternal Son of God in human flesh and the Savior of the world. He is the only one who can save us from sin, and the only way to the Father (John 14:6). All who reject Him are doomed to suffer eternally for despising the Lord of life and His offer of forgiveness.

Everything hinges on the Resurrection. Along with His atoning death on the Cross, the Lord's rising from the dead is the only means by which people can be forgiven of their sins and our only hope for eternal life. If Jesus rose, He is the Son of God and Christianity is true. Consequently, critics and skeptics have tried desperately to develop alternative theories to explain away the Resurrection. In their vain search for a legitimate alternative, they have demonstrated that they understand the centrality of this doctrine better than some Christians, or at least that they are more concerned about it. Ironically, as will be demonstrated in the coming chapters, the critical and skeptical arguments have actually strengthened our confidence in the truth of the Resurrection.

Conclusion

The apostles knew that Jesus died on the Cross, and just a few days later, they saw Him alive again. They were so sure of this fact that they were willing to face persecution, exile, and death. Imagine having a confidence in the Resurrection similar to the

---

[3] Philip Schaff and David Schley Schaff, *History of the Christian Church* (New York: Charles Scribner's Sons, 1910), I.2.19.
[4] Gary R. Habermas and Michael R. Licona, *The Case for the Resurrection of Jesus* (Grand Rapids, MI: Kregel Publications, 2004), p. 183.

apostles. What would it do to your Christian walk if you had complete assurance of this event? Would you be more motivated than ever to study His Word, spend time in prayer, fellowship with His people, and share the gospel with others?

You are about to embark on a study of the historicity of the Resurrection of Jesus Christ. The next few chapters will examine the evidences for the Resurrection. We will look at what the Bible calls "infallible proofs," essentially surveying the post-Resurrection appearances. This will be followed by a study of several evidences stated in the biblical accounts or derived from them, as well as some evidences from outside of Scripture. We will then turn our attention to the numerous alternative views proposed by skeptics and critics throughout the centuries. By the time we complete our study, you will see that in nearly 2,000 years, not one alternate theory can stand up to scrutiny or come close to accounting for the facts. The final section of the book will address many of the questions and concerns that have been raised about the events surrounding the Resurrection and whether Christians should even celebrate the holiday often called Easter.

2 What Are the "Infallible Proofs" of the Resurrection?

The previous chapter explained the importance of the Resurrection of Jesus to the Christian faith. Its centrality is shown by the fact that believing Jesus rose from the dead is essential for salvation. For example, in his letter to the Romans, Paul stated "that if you confess with your mouth the Lord Jesus and believe in your heart that God has raised Him from the dead, you will be saved" (Romans 10:9; cf. 1 Corinthians 15:12–21). So, does belief in this all-important miracle stem from blind faith or do Christians have good reasons for believing that the Resurrection was a real event in history?

When we start from God's Word, there is absolutely no legitimate way to deny the angel's words to the women who came to the tomb on that glorious morning: "Why do you seek the living among the dead? He is not here but is risen!" (Luke 24:5–6). The Bible repeatedly affirms the bodily Resurrection of Jesus, even stating that He demonstrated it "by many infallible proofs" (Acts 1:3). What are some of these infallible proofs? Are there any other good arguments consistent with this belief?

Infallible Proofs

In the "prologue" to the book of Acts, Luke told Theophilus that Jesus "presented Himself alive after His suffering by many infallible proofs, being seen by them during forty days and speaking of the things pertaining to the kingdom of God" (Acts 1:3).

The Greek word translated as "infallible proofs" is τεκμηρίοις (*tekmēriois*), a technical term from logic[1] that refers to that which causes something "to be known in a convincing and decisive manner, *proof*" (italics in original).[2] Another lexicon defines it as "that which causes something to be known as verified or confirmed—'evidence, proof, convincing proof.'"[3] It is a *hapax legomenon*, meaning that it only appears once in Scripture, but it is found in other Greek writings where it also referred to a "sure sign or token," a "proof," or in the logic of Aristotle, a "demonstrative proof."[4]

So just what are these "infallible proofs" of the Resurrection? Before answering that question, consider what it would take to convince you that someone was alive again after dying. Of course, the best evidence would be an opportunity to spend time with that person again—you could see him walk and talk, and you could eat with him. That's precisely what Luke is referring to here. After being crucified, Jesus showed Himself alive by appearing to the disciples on several occasions. He walked with them, talked with them, and ate with them.

Combining the data from various New Testament books, we know that Jesus appeared to some of His followers on at least ten occasions before ascending to heaven. Determining the order of the following appearances is beyond the scope of this chapter, so I have listed them according to the arrangement described in chapter 19.

- Mary Magdalene (John 20:11–18)
- The other Mary, Salome, Joanna, and at least one other woman (Matthew 28:1; Mark 16:1; Luke 24:10)

---

[1] John B. Polhill, *Acts: The New American Commentary, vol. 26* (Nashville: Broadman & Holman Publishers, 1995), p. 81.

[2] Walter Bauer, William F. Arndt, F. Wilbur Gingrich, and Frederick W. Danker, (*BDAG*) *A Greek-English Lexicon of the New Testament and Other Early Christian Literature*, 3rd ed., revised and edited by Frederick W. Danker (Chicago, IL: University of Chicago Press, 2001), s.v. "τεκμήριον," p. 994.

[3] Johannes P. Louw and Eugene Albert Nida, vol. 1, *Greek-English Lexicon of the New Testament: Based on Semantic Domains*, electronic ed. of the 2nd edition. (New York: United Bible Societies, 1996), p. 339.

[4] Henry George Liddell and Robert Scott, *A Greek-English Lexicon, with a revised supplement 1996* (Oxford: Clarendon Press, 1843, 1996), p. 1768.

- Peter (Luke 24:34; 1 Corinthians 15:5)
- Cleopas and another disciple on road to Emmaus (Luke 24:13-35)
- The eleven disciples minus Thomas (Luke 24:36-43; John 20:19-25)
- The eleven disciples (John 20:26-29)
- Seven disciples at the Sea of Tiberias (John 21:1-23)
- Disciples at a mountain in Galilee (Matthew 28:16-17)
- James (1 Corinthians 15:7)
- Disciples, possibly in Jerusalem before He led them to the Mt. of Olives, gave the Great Commission, and ascended into heaven (Luke 24:49-53; Acts 1:3-11)

In most instances, we are told that Jesus did more than just appear before people. Christ's words in John 20:17 seem to imply that Mary Magdalene clung to Him, indicating that He could be touched. The other women worshiped Him and held Him by the feet (Matthew 28:9). He broke bread in front of Cleopas and an unnamed follower (Luke 24:30). He showed the scars in His hands, feet, and side and then ate fish and a honeycomb before the gathering of disciples without Thomas (Luke 24:40-43; John 20:20). Later, with Thomas present, Jesus invited Thomas to touch His hands and His side (John 20:26-27). At the Sea of Tiberias, He performed a miracle, allowing the disciples to catch 153 large fish (John 20:6-11). He also cooked and ate some food (John 20:9, 15). Paul stated that Jesus had appeared to over 500 people at one time (1 Corinthians 15:6). This may be an additional appearance, or it may be the same event as the one on the hillside in Galilee (Matthew 28:16-17).

The report in 1 Corinthians 15 is probably the earliest extant writing about the Resurrection appearances, penned around AD 55. Paul claimed that he was writing what he had received. What was the source of the message that Paul preached? It could have been given to him directly by Jesus (Galatians 1:12), although here he was probably referring to his meetings with Peter and James in Jerusalem within five years of the Crucifixion and Resurrection (Galatians 1:18-19). Paul wrote that he went to "see Peter" (v. 18). The word translated as "see" is from the root ἱστορέω (historeō), which refers to inquiring for the purpose of coming to know someone or something,[5] and from which we derive our English word *history*.[6] So Paul told the Galatians that he not only received his message from Jesus, but also had it confirmed by Peter and James. Even the critical scholars acknowledge that Paul received this teaching within a few years of the death of Jesus.[7]

Some skeptics claim that the idea of the Resurrection was simply a legend that grew for several decades before being written down. First Corinthians 15:1–9 smashes this objection. Not only is five years much too short a time for such a legend to develop, but Paul cites a bunch of eyewitnesses "most of whom [were] still alive" (1 Corinthians 15:6, ESV). Essentially, he told the Corinthians, "Hey, if you don't believe me, then go ask one of these guys." The idea that the Resurrection was the product of legend is further examined in chapter 7.

So are the appearances truly "infallible proofs" of the Resurrection? They certainly were for the people who saw Him. Luke wasn't alone in thinking of the appearances in such a manner. Paul told the Greek philosophers who gathered in the Areopagus in Athens that God had "furnished proof to all men by raising [Jesus] from the dead" (Acts 17:31). "Proof" is from the Greek πίστιν (*pistin*) and refers to "a token offered as a guarantee of something promised." It is a "proof" or "pledge."[8]

Jesus said on multiple occasions that His death and Resurrection would be the one sign He would give to an unbelieving and wicked generation. When asked by the Jews to perform a sign, He predicted His Resurrection by saying, "Destroy this temple, and in three days I will raise it up" (John 2:19–22). Later, some scribes and Pharisees asked Him for a sign, and Jesus replied, "An evil and adulterous generation seeks after a sign, and no sign will be given to it except the sign of the prophet Jonah. For as Jonah was three days and three nights in the belly of the great fish, so will

[5] *BDAG*, s.v. "ἱστορέω", p. 483.
[6] Michael R. Licona, *The Resurrection of Jesus: A New Historiographical Approach* (Downers Grove, IL: IVP Academic, 2010), p. 230.
[7] Gary R. Habermas and Michael R. Licona, *The Case for the Resurrection of Jesus* (Grand Rapids, MI: Kregel Publications, 2004), pp. 52–53.
[8] *BDAG*, s.v., πίστις, p. 818.

the Son of Man be three days and three nights in the heart of the earth" (Matthew 12:39–40). He gave a similar response to such a request in Matthew 16:1–4 as well.

In one of His debates with the Pharisees, Jesus said, "It is also written in your law that the testimony of two men is true" (John 8:17). This oft-repeated concept refers back to Deuteronomy 19:15—"by the mouth of two or three witnesses the matter shall be established." This same idea is at the heart of the American judicial system. Witnesses appear in trials to help establish the truth of the matter. Prior to the use of modern forensic experts and recording devices, reliable eyewitnesses were essential. People believe in the historicity of many past events because of eyewitness testimony without ever seeing photographic evidence for those events.

Multiple reliable eyewitnesses testified that Jesus was alive after being dead and buried. Some of these eyewitness accounts have been preserved for us in the Bible, and because this is the inspired and inerrant Word of God, Scripture is actually another infallible proof of Christ's Resurrection. Nevertheless, many people still refuse to believe because of the hardness of their hearts.

The Heart of Unbelief

Some may wonder how a proof could be called infallible when so many people refuse to believe it. In the case of the risen Jesus, the problem was not with the evidence. After all, He was standing in front of them and could be touched and heard.[9] Even today, the problem is not with the infallible proof of Scripture, nor is there a problem with the evidence from history or archaeology. The main problem is with humanity's stubbornly rebellious heart. Jesus spoke to this issue when talking about the rich man and Lazarus (Luke 16:19–31). The rich man in Hades pleaded with Abraham in glory to send Lazarus back from the dead to warn the rich man's brothers about the torments that awaited them if they didn't repent. He claimed that "if one goes to them from

---

[9] It should be noted that while some people reject the inerrant record (the Bible) of the infallible proofs, a study of the historical evidences for the Resurrection of Jesus has been a major factor in some people coming to faith in Christ, including apologists like C.S. Lewis, Josh McDowell, and Lee Strobel.

the dead, they will repent" (v. 30). Abraham's response alludes to Christ's Resurrection and illustrates the stubbornness of the sinner's heart: "If they do not hear Moses and the prophets, neither will they be persuaded though one rise from the dead" (v. 31).[10] This willful rejection of the truth is well illustrated by a series of quotations from atheist philosopher Michael Martin concerning the evidence for Christ's Resurrection.

> "It is not inconceivable that on very rare occasions someone being restored to life has no natural or supernatural cause"; "I admit that some events could occur without any cause"; "[E]ven if the resurrection of Jesus was justified by the evidence, it would not support the belief that the Christian God exists and that Jesus is the Son of God."[11]

In an effort to escape the implications of the Resurrection, Martin is willing to reject one of the fundamental principles of scientific methodology: cause and effect. Instead of bowing the knee to His Creator, Martin would rather believe in a causeless effect by which, out of all the people who have ever lived, the one who just happened to come back to life for no reason at all was Jesus, the Man who had fulfilled numerous Old Testament prophecies, lived a sinless life, performed countless miracles, and predicted His own Resurrection (Matthew 20:18–19). This is special pleading at its worst.

Martin's statement provides a great example of how a person usually interprets the data according to his worldview. As an atheist, Martin is prepared to believe just about anything on this matter except that God raised Jesus from the dead. When a person desires to remain in his skepticism, he will develop excuses to disbelieve the obvious. Although the Resurrection of Jesus Christ was proven by "many infallible proofs" and has been recorded in God's Word, atheists like Michael Martin will continue to reject the free gift of God's grace and cling to their irrational, humanistic worldview.

---

[10] Jesus may have also had the raising of Lazarus in mind when He spoke these words. See chapter 21 for details.

[11] Michael Martin, *The Case Against Christianity* (Philadelphia, PA: Temple University Press, 1991), pp. 76, 87, 100, cited in Licona, *The Resurrection of Jesus*, p. 608.

Conclusion

Christians can have the utmost confidence in the death, burial, and Resurrection of Jesus since God's Word accurately tells us about these historical events. These central truths of the Christian faith were also witnessed by hundreds of people. Jesus was publicly executed on a Cross, buried in Joseph's tomb (Mark 15:42–47), and seen alive again by more than 500 people at the same time. To those who saw the risen Savior, the post-Resurrection appearances of Jesus were infallible proofs that He conquered the grave. Today, God's Word is the infallible proof of the event, and those who believe in Him without having seen Him are blessed (John 20:29).

3 Did Jesus Appear to Any Skeptics?

The previous chapter discussed the "many infallible proofs" (Acts 1:3) of the Resurrection. The post-Resurrection appearances of Jesus were enough to persuade His followers that He conquered death. Skeptics have claimed that since the alleged appearances were only to His followers, it shows that they simply made up the story. They say that if He would have appeared to some unbelievers and they became His followers, then the accounts would be more credible. What are we to make of this claim? Did Jesus ever appear to someone who was not already His follower?

Conversion of James

The man who wrote the Epistle of James was the half-brother of Jesus, the son of Mary and Joseph. Since there are at least four people named James mentioned in the New Testament, how can we be sure which man wrote the letter? The solution is actually not very difficult.

James the son of Zebedee could not have written this letter since he was martyred around AD 44 (Acts 12:2), which is probably before the writing of this epistle. The authoritative tone of the epistle and the implication of the introduction that James was well known likely rules out the obscure James the Less and the James of Luke 6:16. The only other James in the NT was one of several sons of Mary and Joseph (Mark 6:3). He was in the upper room with Mary and his brothers on the Day of Pentecost (Acts 1:14) and became a leader of the church in Jerusalem in the early years (Acts 12:17, 15:13, 21:18). The fact that in this epistle he calls himself the bondservant of the Lord Jesus Christ (James 1:1) reflects his understanding that his spiritual connection to Jesus is far more important than their familial relationship.

For whatever reason, James did not believe in Jesus as the Messiah prior to the Resurrection. In fact, none of His brothers believed in Him early on (John 7:5). On one occasion they even tried to prevent Him from speaking, thinking He was out of His mind (Mark 3:20–21, NET). However, just several weeks after the Crucifixion they were counted among His followers (Acts 1:14). And by the time of the "Jerusalem Council" in Acts 15, James was one of the leading figures at the church in Jerusalem. Paul implies this as well in Galatians 1:18–19, 2:9, calling James one of the "pillars" of the church.

Several early sources reveal that James was eventually martyred for his faith, although they are not in complete agreement about how he was killed. Josephus reported that James was stoned as a lawbreaker.[1] Eusebius, citing Clement, stated that James "was thrown from the pinnacle of the temple and was beaten to death with the club by a fuller."[2] Later, Eusebius cites Hegesippus, "who lived immediately after the apostles," for an account of the death of James that combines elements from Josephus and Clement. According to this report, James was thrown off the temple pinnacle but survived the fall, so the Jews began to stone him until a fuller struck him on the head with a club.[3] If the latter account is accurate, then there is no contradiction. However, no matter which view is correct, they all agree on the main point: James was martyred for his faith in Jesus.

What could possibly compel a man who had grown up with Jesus to suddenly change his mind about his older brother? James likely remained in his unbelief until after Christ's death. After all, while Jesus was on the Cross, He entrusted the care of His mother to the Apostle John (John 19:26–27). If one of his brothers had been a believer at this point, it would have been their responsibility to care for Mary. Although Scripture does not describe the conversion of James for us, it does provide the

---

[1] Josephus, *Antiquities of the Jews*, 20.200.
[2] Eusebius, *Ecclesiastical History*, 2.1.5.
[3] Ibid., 2.23.11–18.

most likely catalyst for his drastic change of heart. Upon telling his readers that Jesus appeared to over 500 people at once, Paul wrote, "After that He was seen by James" (1 Corinthians 15:7).

While it is possible that James converted to the faith based on reports of his brother's Resurrection, it is far more likely that he became a believer when Jesus appeared to him. Whatever it was that triggered his conversion, the one-time skeptic James believed in the Resurrection so strongly that he was willing to die for his faith.

Finally, it is helpful to see how unbelievers handle the relationship between Jesus and His brothers. Skeptics often emphasize the negative reactions from His family in their efforts to show that Jesus was not viewed by anyone—not even His own family—as the Son of God. On the other hand, many critical scholars, such as John Painter, Richard Bauckham, and James Tabor, have attempted to downplay the resistance Jesus faced from His own family. This deemphasizing of the opposition He faced is likely due to their attempts to portray Jesus as less confrontational and more "tolerant" of sinners. Also, it allows them to discount the appearance to James as a major factor in his conversion, since these scholars often hold to some form of spiritual resurrection.[4] In both cases, we see unbelievers attempting to misuse Scripture to suit their desires rather than simply allowing the eyewitnesses to explain what really happened.

Conversion of Saul/Paul

The Apostle Paul (also called Saul) is responsible for penning at least 13 books of the New Testament and is arguably the most influential Christian ever. But he was not always a devout follower of Christ. We are first introduced to him observing the stoning of Stephen (Acts 7:58). A few verses later we read that Saul "made havoc of the church, entering every house, and dragging off men and women, committing them to prison" (Acts 8:3). He would later tell an angry crowd in Jerusalem that he persecuted Christians "to the death, binding and delivering into prisons both men and

---

[4] For a critique of the arguments used by Painter, Bauckham, and Tabor, see Michael R. Licona, *The Resurrection of Jesus*, pp. 440–455.

women" (Acts 22:4). He wrote that he "persecuted the church of God beyond measure and tried to destroy it" (Galatians 1:13).

From a human perspective, this is not the person we would select to carry the gospel message throughout the Roman Empire, but God had other plans for Paul. Acts 9 opens with the following words: "Then Saul, still breathing threats and murder against the disciples of the Lord, went to the high priest and asked letters from him to the synagogues of Damascus, so that if he found any who were of the Way, whether men or women, he might bring them bound to Jerusalem" (Acts 9:1–2). Paul was the church's greatest persecutor, but he was about to see the Light, pun intended.

As Paul approached Damascus, Jesus appeared to him and asked, "Saul, Saul, why are you persecuting Me?" (Acts 9:4). Upon seeing the risen Savior, Saul converted to the Christian faith and tirelessly preached the gospel—Christ's death for sins, burial, and Resurrection—until his martyrdom many years later. The apostle described some of the trials he endured for Christ:

> … in labors more abundant, in stripes above measure, in prisons more frequently, in deaths often. From the Jews five times I received forty stripes minus one. Three times I was beaten with rods; once I was stoned; three times I was shipwrecked; a night and a day I have been in the deep; in journeys often, in perils of waters, in perils of robbers, in perils of my own countrymen, in perils of the Gentiles, in perils in the city, in perils in the wilderness, in perils in the sea, in perils among false brethren, in weariness and toil, in sleeplessness often, in hunger and thirst, in fastings often, in cold and nakedness . . . (2 Corinthians 11:23–27)

What could possibly explain such a drastic change of heart? This was not a foolish man swayed by poor argumentation, nor was he prone to changing his views based on shifting public opinion. Paul was a scholar and a well-respected Pharisee. But he was suddenly transformed into a fearless evangelist and church planter who suffered greatly for preaching the gospel before Jews and Gentiles, kings, civil leaders, and commoners.

The only reasonable explanation for this change of heart is precisely what Paul said it was: "Then last of all [Jesus] was seen by me also" (1 Corinthians 15:8). Paul was so committed to serving Christ that he was beheaded in Rome during Nero's reign.[5] His treatise on the absolute necessity of the Resurrection for the Christian faith in 1 Corinthians 15 demonstrates this former Pharisee's undying commitment to the gospel of Christ.

Conclusion

After conquering the grave, Jesus appeared to more than 500 people. At least two of these people were skeptical of His claims before they met the risen Lord, but they certainly were not skeptical after the fact. Both were willing to die for their belief that Jesus rose from the dead. There may have been other skeptics who converted upon seeing the risen Christ, but we are not specifically told about them. Nevertheless, the critics' claim that Jesus only appeared to His followers does not stand up to scrutiny.

So far we have looked at the post-Resurrection appearances of Jesus as "infallible proofs" of the event. The following chapter will survey many more evidences that corroborate the eyewitness accounts recorded for us in Scripture.

---

[5] Eusebius, *Ecclesiastical History*, 2.25.5.

4 What Are Some Other Evidences of the Resurrection?

So far we have discussed the appearances Jesus made to His disciples and to a couple of former skeptics. There are many more evidences we need to survey to demonstrate the wide array of support for the Resurrection that can be marshalled. Some of these evidences are explicitly stated in the text, while others are based on strong inferences drawn from it. As such, certain points are more compelling than others, but taken together with the "infallible proofs," there is only one reasonable conclusion: Jesus rose physically from the dead.

The Change in the Disciples

James and Paul were not the only people to undergo drastic changes upon encountering the risen Savior. On the night Jesus was arrested, His disciples fled in fear (Mark 14:50). As far as we know, of the eleven disciples only John had the courage to remain close enough to Jesus to observe some of the proceedings up to and including the Crucifixion (John 18:15, 19:26). Peter attempted to stay with Jesus but ended up denying Christ several times before fleeing in shame (Matthew 26:69–75).

Less than two months later, Peter stood in front of thousands of Jews in Jerusalem and boldly delivered one of the least "seeker-sensitive" messages of all time. He declared that they had "taken by lawless hands, [had] crucified, and put to death" their Messiah, but "God raised [Him] up" (Acts 2:23). It's difficult to imagine how offensive Peter's words would have been to such a crowd. These people had been longing for the Messiah to come, but when He came, they failed to recognize Him (Luke 19:41–44; Acts 3:17; 1 Corinthians 2:8). Instead of welcoming Him with open arms, they had delivered Him to be executed by one of the most brutal means imaginable—crucifixion.

But Peter and the disciples weren't done. After healing a crippled man in the name of Jesus, Peter soon spoke to another large crowd of Jews in the temple. He unflinchingly proclaimed, "But you denied the Holy One and the Just, and asked for a murderer to be granted to you, and killed the Prince of life, whom God raised from the dead, of which we are witnesses" (Acts 3:14–15).

The disciples were arrested, and on the next day they stood before "their rulers, elders, and scribes, as well as Annas the high priest, [and] Caiaphas..." (Acts 4:5–6). What was Peter's message? "Let it be known to you all, and to the people of Israel, that by the name of Jesus Christ of Nazareth, whom you crucified, whom God raised from the dead, by Him this man stands here before you whole... Nor is there salvation in any other, for there is no other name under heaven given among men by which we must be saved" (vv. 10, 12). The disciples were commanded by the authorities to stop preaching in the name of Jesus (v. 4:18), but they replied, "Whether it is right in the sight of God to listen to you more than to God, you judge. For we cannot but speak the things which we have seen and heard" (vv. 4:19–20). Upon their release and following a prayer for boldness, we are told, "And with great power the apostles gave witness to the resurrection of the Lord Jesus" (Acts 4:33).

In the next chapter of Acts, the disciples were arrested and imprisoned, miraculously freed by an angel, and taken into custody again. They refused to stop preaching and told the council, "We ought to obey God rather than men. The God of our fathers raised up Jesus whom you murdered by hanging on a tree" (Acts 5:30).

According to church tradition, all of the disciples except for John suffered a martyr's death because they continually preached what they had seen and heard: Jesus was crucified, but now He was alive again because God had raised Him from the dead. James, the brother of John, was killed by Herod with the sword (Acts 12:2). An early church tradition records that Peter was crucified upside down, which is consistent with what Jesus told him in John 21:18-19. Early church tradition also holds that the other disciples suffered martyrdom in various manners: spearing, flaying, crucifixion, the sword, and boiling in oil.

The book of Acts makes it pretty clear why these men who fled in fear on the night Jesus was arrested were willing to die for Him. They were filled with the Spirit (Acts 2:4, 4:8), and they knew that even though Jesus had died, He was alive and well. They had seen Him with their own eyes and touched Him with their own hands (1 John 1:1-3), and only death could silence them.

Liars Don't Make Good Martyrs

Scoffers have attempted to downplay this remarkable proof of the Resurrection by claiming that many people are willing to die for a cause. For example, some Muslims are willing to blow themselves up to kill Jews. That's true, but it misses the point. The Muslims who do this sort of thing sincerely *believe* in their cause, but they do not *know* if it's true. The disciples were in a position to know whether or not Jesus was raised from the dead. It simply is not plausible to suggest that each of these men would face continual persecution and horrifying deaths for something they *knew* to be a lie. After all, liars don't make good martyrs.

Furthermore, in contrast to suicide bombers, the disciples didn't kill others in their respective martyrdoms. And they didn't use violence to force people to convert to Christianity. In fact, they did no harm to anyone, but loved their enemies and willingly accepted persecution from them for the sake of the gospel. It is a sad fact of history that centuries later some who claimed to be Christians killed others and died in war in attempts to advance the Christian faith (e.g., in the Crusades of the eleventh through thirteenth centuries). But such behavior is completely contrary to the teachings and examples of Jesus Christ and His apostles.

The Empty Tomb

Jesus was buried in the tomb of a council member from Arimathea named Joseph (John 19:38–42). All four Gospels testify to this fact. The tomb was guarded by Roman soldiers, and a Roman seal was affixed to it (Matthew 27:62–66). If Jesus was bodily resurrected from the dead, then we would expect that His body would not remain in the tomb. Of course, that's precisely what was discovered on the Sunday morning after the Crucifixion—His body was gone and only the burial cloths remained.

As we will see in upcoming chapters, the fact that the tomb was empty has led to numerous imaginative alternative views. If the Lord's body was still in the tomb on the Day of Pentecost when Peter preached in Jerusalem, the Jewish leaders could have grabbed Peter, taken him to the tomb, and said, "Look, there's Jesus. He didn't rise from the dead. Now stop lying to everyone about it." Yet there is not a single ancient record of this sort. Instead, the Jewish leaders who opposed Christianity invented the incredible idea that the disciples stole the body to explain away the empty tomb (Matthew 28:11–15). It is important to note that not all of the Jewish people or their leaders were opposed to Peter's preaching. After all, the earliest church was made up almost entirely of Jews. Three thousand Jews converted after his Pentecost proclamation (Acts 2:41). It soon grew to 5,000 (Acts 4:4), and "then the word of God spread, and the number of the disciples multiplied greatly in Jerusalem, and a *great many of the priests* were obedient to the faith" (Acts 6:7, emphasis added).

The fact that the opponents of the early Christians acknowledged the empty tomb lends authenticity to the accounts, since a person's enemies are unlikely to help him make his case. This is known as the principle of enemy attestation or the testimony of a hostile witness. "If opponents of the eyewitnesses admit certain facts the eyewitnesses say are true, then those facts probably are true (for example, if your mother says you are brave, that might be true; but it's probably more credible if your archenemy says the same thing)."[1]

---

[1] Norman L. Geisler and Frank Turek, *I Don't Have Enough Faith to Be an Atheist* (Wheaton, IL: Crossway Books, 2004), p. 231.

The Existence of the Church

As noted in the first chapter, Philip Schaff stated, "The Christian church rests on the resurrection of its Founder. Without this fact the church could never have been born, or if born, it would soon have died a natural death."[2] After an exhaustive study of early Christian beliefs about the Resurrection, N.T. Wright wrote, "Christianity is inexplicable apart from the assumption that virtually all early Christians . . . did indeed believe that Jesus of Nazareth had been raised bodily from the dead."[3]

Due to the remarkable circumstances in first-century Jerusalem, Christianity would never have been able to get started if Jesus had not risen from the dead. Recall that the Resurrection of Jesus was central to the disciples' preaching. Even if they had the courage to preach without having seen the risen Lord, what message would they have proclaimed? They certainly could not repeatedly claim to have been eyewitnesses of His Resurrection, as they did (Acts 2:32, 3:15, 5:32, 10:39, 13:31). Without this bold proclamation of the Resurrection, and if His body was rotting in the grave, people would not be converted and the memory of Jesus and His disciples would quickly fade. In fact, it may be safely said that if Jesus did not rise from the dead, very few people living today, if any, would have ever heard of Him.[4]

Undivided Testimony of New Testament

As could be expected, the New Testament writers were undivided in their proclamation that Jesus rose from the dead. Space does not permit an exhaustive treatment of the subject here, but consider that the Resurrection is explicitly mentioned in every New Testament book except for the short letters of Philemon, James, 2 Peter, 2 John, 3 John, and Jude. Yet even these letters presume the truth of the Resurrection since Jesus is portrayed as living and active. From the penning of the earliest

[2] Philip Schaff and David Schley Schaff, *History of the Christian Church*, I.2.19.
[3] N.T. Wright, *The Resurrection of the Son of God* (Minneapolis, MN: Fortress Press, 2003), p. 587.
[4] For more reasons why Christianity could not exist as we know it if Jesus did not rise, see James P. Holding, *The Impossible Faith: Why Christianity Succeeded when It Should Have Failed* (Longwood, FL: Xulon Press, 2007).

New Testament book to the final one, the Resurrection of Jesus is consistently viewed as central to Christian teaching.

Principle of Embarrassment

A key idea used by historians in weighing the historical validity of alleged events has been called the principle of embarrassment. That is, if the writer included details that would seem to hurt his position, then those details are likely true, since one would not readily undercut his own beliefs with certain data that could just as easily be left unreported.[5] Applied to the topic at hand, this principle does not directly relate to the Resurrection, but it is indirectly related since it provides multiple clues that the eyewitness accounts are authentic.

The Bible includes numerous embarrassing details about its leading figures. For example, David was an adulterer and murderer (2 Samuel 11). Peter was accused of being a mouthpiece of Satan by Jesus when Peter denied that Jesus would be killed in Jerusalem and rise again (Matthew 16:23). Later, despite his promises to the contrary, Peter denied Jesus several times (Luke 22:31–35, 54–62). When it comes to the Resurrection accounts in the Gospels, the writers include some embarrassing details that actually afford credibility to their extraordinary claim that Jesus rose from the dead.

If the disciples were inventing Christianity, as has been alleged by some critics and skeptics, then surely they could have made up a more respectable story. They could have claimed that the first witnesses of the empty tomb and the risen Christ were esteemed men like Nicodemus, Joseph of Arimathea, and perhaps some other members of the Sanhedrin. Maybe they could have said that Jesus appeared to Herod, Pilate, or even the emperor himself. That would be impressive. But what does Scripture tell us about the first witnesses of these things? They were women—at least five of them traveled to the tomb early on Easter morning (Luke 24:10). Given that a woman's testimony was not highly valued in that

---

[5] Geisler and Turek, p. 231, 275. See also Gary R. Habermas and Michael R. Licona, *The Case for the Resurrection of Jesus* (Grand Rapids, MI: Kregel Publications, 2004), p. 40.

patriarchal society,[6] it would make no sense for the writers to include this detail if they were attempting to gain a following—unless it was true.

This information is even more embarrassing when we consider who the very first eyewitness was. Who in their right mind would ever make up the idea that Mary Magdalene was the first person to see the risen Savior? By this time Mary was surely a devoted follower of Christ, but she would have virtually zero credibility with anyone outside of the disciples' circle, and even they didn't initially believe her report (Luke 24:11). After all, this was a woman "out of whom had come seven demons" (Luke 8:4).[7] That the biblical writers assign Mary Magdalene as the first eyewitness of the resurrected Christ lends strong support for the truthfulness of the account.

Lack of Sensationalism

The straightforward reporting of the Gospel writers adds tremendous weight to their authenticity. Certain skeptics have claimed that the Resurrection accounts are the result of legendary development. But if this were true we should expect to find clear-cut examples of sensationalistic details. Consider the pseudepigraphal book known as the *Gospel of Peter*. Commonly dated to the latter half of the second century AD, this "Gospel" claims that two angels walk out of the tomb with Jesus and are followed by a floating cross. The bodies of the angels and Jesus stretch above the clouds and then the cross actually speaks by answering affirmatively that it had preached to those who sleep. This is the stuff of legend, yet the Resurrection accounts in the canonical Gospels do not contain this type of bizarre activity.

---

[6] Gerald L. Borchert, *John 12–21: The New American Commentary*, vol. 25b (Nashville, TN: Broadman & Holman Publishers, 2002), p. 297.

[7] Although Mary Magdalene is often thought of as a former prostitute, the Bible never directly identifies her as such. This tradition apparently started when Pope Gregory announced this idea in a homily in AD 591. This seems to have been an honest mistake made by conflating the sinful woman who washed Christ's feet with her tears at the end of Luke 7 with Mary Magdalene, who is mentioned early in Luke 8. While it is possible that Mary was the woman in Luke 7, this is more than the text states. Certainly, the labeling of Mary Magdalene as a prostitute was not part of a sinister smear campaign launched by the early church to defame Mary Magdalene, as popularized in Dan Brown's best-selling novel, *The Da Vinci Code*. If that were the Roman Catholic Church's intention, it is indeed strange that they would venerate Mary Magdalene as a saint and honor her with a feast day each year on July 22.

Another interesting detail that lends credibility to the Gospels is the fact that not a single individual is said to have witnessed the actual event of Jesus rising from the dead. If the Gospel writers were making up the event, they sure missed out on the most obvious "proof" they could have invented. They wrote about the most important and dramatic event in history and not a single person was there to watch it happen. Surely Matthew or Mark could have placed a respected man like Nicodemus or Joseph of Arimathea at the tomb to watch Christ rise or at least to witness Him coming out of the tomb. But these details are not recorded because the Gospel writers did not make up the event. Instead they accurately recorded what actually happened.

While discussing this subject, people often ask if there are any evidences of the Resurrection from outside of the Bible. While Scripture is perfectly reliable, it is helpful to understand that extra-biblical evidences are consistent with the Bible.

The Nazareth Inscription

An interesting archaeological discovery lends early support to the truth of the biblical accounts of the Resurrection. The Nazareth Inscription is a marble tablet with Greek writing that has been dated to sometime in the AD 40s. The inscription is likely a rescript, an abbreviated form of an edict, from Emperor Claudius.

The wording of this particular find indicates that the message of the Resurrection, or at least the Jewish response to it, had been brought to the emperor's attention within about ten years of the event. In just fourteen brief lines this rescript explains a new law carrying capital punishment for anyone who would move a body from graves or tombs to another place with wicked intent. That is, no one was permitted to move an entombed body for fraudulent reasons.

Why is this so intriguing? Think about the response of the Jewish leaders to the Resurrection reports. They bribed the Roman soldiers to say, "His disciples came at night and stole Him away while we slept" (Matthew 28:13). Why would the Roman emperor issue an edict forbidding the moving of a body with fraudulent intent? Sure, there were grave robbers at that time, but grave robbers weren't interested in stealing bodies—they wanted the valuables occasionally buried with the body. Interestingly enough, there is no mention of valuables in the edict, but there is a comment forbidding the moving of sepulcher-sealing stones. These types of stones were only used in Israel, so the wording of this edict pinpoints the reason for its issuance. Something had happened in Israel concerning the reported moving of a body that had caused enough ripples throughout the empire to merit the attention of the emperor.

The Nazareth Inscription does not prove that Jesus rose from the dead, but it is consistent with the biblical accounts. It also gives extra-biblical testimony to the growing impact of the church and its central message of the Resurrection soon after Christ's death.[8]

The Shroud of Turin?

Some Christians believe that the Shroud of Turin was the actual burial cloth of Jesus and provides evidence of both His Crucifixion and Resurrection, but this claim is rejected by many Christians who believe the Shroud to be an elaborate hoax from medieval times. This 14-foot long cloth bears faint images of the front and back of a man, complete with all of the marks consistent with the torture Jesus endured during His last hours. Adequately dealing with the Shroud would require several chapters. I am not fully persuaded one way or the other about it, but if the Shroud contradicts the biblical account in any way, then it cannot be the burial cloth of Christ nor could it be used as evidence for the Resurrection.[9]

---

[8] For more details on this fascinating discovery, along with a full translation of its inscription, please see "The Nazareth Inscription: Proof of the Resurrection of Christ?" available at www.biblearchaeology.org/post/2009/07/22/The-Nazareth-Inscription-Proof-of-the-Resurrection-of-Christ.aspx.

[9] For an overview of some of the reasons why the Shroud of Turin is so intriguing and does not necessarily contradict Scripture, see my blog post titled, "The Ever-Intriguing Shroud of Turin" at <www.midwestapologetics.org/blog/?p=946>. For detailed studies on the Shroud of Turin, see Kenneth E. Stevenson and Gary R. Habermas, *The Shroud and the Controversy* (Nasvhille, TN: Thomas Nelson, 1990), and Ian Wilson, *The Shroud: The 2000-Year-Old Mystery Solved* (London: Bantam Press, 2010).

Subjective Evidences

My favorite song as a young boy mentions a remarkable, though subjective evidence that Jesus is alive today. The chorus of "He Lives" closes with the words, "You ask me how I know He lives, He lives within my heart." This may sound strange to an unbeliever, but Christians can testify to significant, positive life-change as a result of trusting in the risen Christ. People from every nation, from all walks of life, all levels of age or education or material prosperity, all religious backgrounds, and all kinds of moral or immoral lifestyles can testify to a radical change of values, priorities, relationships, and purpose in life as a result of trusting in Jesus Christ as Savior and Lord. Drunks, violent men, prostitutes, addicts, and filthy perverts have found victory from sin through the Lord Jesus Christ. The Bible explains that by His life-giving Spirit Jesus dwells in the hearts of believers through faith (Ephesians 3:17) to gradually transform their lives to be like Christ (Romans 12:2; 2 Corinthians 3:18, 5:17; Ephesians 2:8–10).

Again, this evidence is subjective, and I wouldn't expect anyone to start believing in the Resurrection based solely on someone's personal experience. But changed lives are exactly what we would expect if the one who claimed to forgive sin and give eternal life in relationship with God really did rise from the dead. Conversely, if Jesus didn't rise from the dead, it is very difficult to explain so many changed lives down through the centuries.

Like James and Paul, other former skeptics have been persuaded that Christianity is true based largely on their attempts to disprove the faith, particularly the Resurrection. Some of the most popular Christian apologists, such as Josh McDowell, Lee Strobel, and C.S. Lewis,[10] have testified that their attempts to disprove the Resurrection of Jesus were integral to their conversion.

---

[10] See "The Evidence for the Resurrection of Jesus Christ Part 1—Can It Persuade Skeptics?" available at <www.philosophy-religion.org/faith/pdfs/resurrection.pdf> for the testimony of McDowell, Lewis, and many others. For Strobel's testimony, see Lee Strobel, "How Easter Killed My Faith in Atheism" available at < http://blogs.wsj.com/speakeasy/2011/04/16/how-easter-killed-my-faith-in-atheism>. Both articles accessed January 20, 2014.

While God is the only one who can supernaturally change a person's heart, He often uses the evidences of the Resurrection to remove intellectual objections to the Christian faith.
John Whitcomb explained that in the account of Jesus raising Lazarus from the dead, it was God who did the supernatural work (raising Lazarus), but He commanded people to move the sepulcher-sealing stone (John 11:39) and unwrap Lazarus (v. 46). Many of the Jews believed in Jesus when they saw this incredible miracle (John 11:45), and the chief priests "plotted to put Lazarus to death also, because on account of him many of the Jews went away and believed in Jesus" (John 12:10–11). In a sense, that's how these evidences for the Resurrection of Christ can be used. Figuratively, we can roll away the stones of objections so that people can see the risen Lord.

Conclusion

The Bible provides numerous lines of evidence that can be used to corroborate the Resurrection of Jesus as a historical event. When combined with the infallible proofs mentioned in chapters 2 and 3, one can build a formidable case that the greatest of miracles occurred that first Easter morning in a tomb outside of Jerusalem. In nearly two millennia the critics have tried desperately to develop a workable alternative that can account for the evidence, yet each alternative proposal has failed miserably as will be shown in the coming chapters. Before addressing these alternate views, we need to spend a chapter looking at what historians have had to say about these evidences.

5 What Do Historians Say About the Evidences of the Resurrection?

The Bible is the Word of God, so it is accurate in all it affirms. Since it tells us Jesus rose from the dead, we can have complete confidence that He did. What many people fail to recognize is that even if we were to use the critics' and skeptics' own criteria, the most reasonable conclusion is the same: Jesus rose from the dead. That is, even if we did not presume biblical authority, and we treated the New Testament as unbelieving historians do, the bodily Resurrection of Jesus is still the only explanation that matches all the accepted facts.

While this methodology is not followed in this book, it is helpful to see how historians from various backgrounds view the data. This chapter will also provide us with a helpful summary of the most widely accepted facts, which will become quite useful in the upcoming critique of the alternative theories. One point will become rather obvious throughout this study: the critics and skeptics simply have an anti-supernatural bias, or more accurately, an anti-biblical bias. Thus, they have developed absurd positions in efforts to explain away the only reasonable conclusion that can be derived from the facts. So what are these facts?

Minimal Facts

Since 1975, Resurrection expert Dr. Gary Habermas has catalogued over 3,400 academic works on the fate of Jesus, from conservative, critical, and skeptical scholars in English, German, and French.

One may be tempted to accuse Habermas of only using material from scholars in his own camp, but his research has actually been skewed to favor the most skeptical positions.

> I endeavored to be more than fair to all the positions. In fact, if anything, I erred in the direction of cataloguing the most radical positions, since this was the only classification where I included even those authors who did not have specialized scholarly credentials or peer-reviewed publications. It is this group, too, that often tends to doubt or deny that Jesus ever existed. Yet, given that I counted many sources in this category, this means that my study is skewed in the skeptical direction far more than if I had stayed strictly with my requirement of citing only those with scholarly credentials. Still, I included these positions quite liberally, even when the wide majority of mainline scholars, "liberals" included, rarely even footnoted this material. Of course, this practice would also skew the numbers who proposed naturalistic theories of the resurrection, to which I particularly gravitated.[1]

From this research Habermas has been able to show that of the 3,400 works studied, the majority of writers accept the following 12 events as historical fact:[2]

1. Jesus died by crucifixion.
2. Jesus was buried.
3. His death caused the disciples to despair and lose hope, believing that his life was ended.
4. The tomb was empty a few days later.
5. The disciples had experiences that they believed were

---

[1] Gary Habermas, "The Minimal Facts Approach to the Resurrection of Jesus: The Role of Methodology as a Crucial Component in Establishing Historicity," *Southeastern Theological Review* 3:1 (Summer 2012): 18. For more information on those who claim that Jesus never existed, see Tim Chaffey, "Feedback: Jesus Did Not Exist." Available at <www.answersingenesis.org/articles/2012/10/26/feedback-jesus-did-not-exist>.

[2] Gary R. Habermas, *The Historical Jesus: Ancient Evidence for the Life of Christ* (Joplin, MO: College Press Publishing Company, 1996), p. 158.

literal appearances of the risen Jesus.

6. The disciples were transformed from doubters who were afraid to identify themselves with Jesus to bold proclaimers of His death and Resurrection.
7. This message was the center of preaching in the early church.
8. This message was especially proclaimed in Jerusalem, where Jesus died and was buried shortly before.
9. The church was born in Jerusalem and grew rapidly.
10. Orthodox Jews who believed in Jesus made Sunday their primary day of worship.
11. James, the half-brother of Jesus, converted to the faith when he saw what he believed was the resurrected Jesus.
12. Paul was converted to the faith after his experience which he believed was with the risen Jesus.

As will be demonstrated in subsequent chapters, if we compare the alternative theories of what happened to the body of Jesus with these 12 facts, we quickly see that none of these views can even come close to matching the evidence. Habermas has gone a step further and reduced this list to just the top five evidences, which he calls the "minimal facts":

1. Jesus died by crucifixion.
2. His disciples believed that He rose and appeared to them.
3. The church persecutor Paul was suddenly changed.
4. The skeptic James, brother of Jesus, was suddenly changed.
5. The tomb was empty.[3]

To make this list, each of these points had to meet two criteria: (1) the data are strongly evidenced, and (2) the data are granted by virtually all scholars on the subject, even the skeptical ones. So even if we were to use the criteria set forth by critical and skeptical scholars, the conclusion that Jesus rose from the dead is still the most reasonable explanation of the facts concerning what happened to His body on that first Easter morning.

[3] Habermas and Licona, *The Case for the Resurrection of Jesus*, pp. 47–77.

In the coming chapters, I will often refer back to these five widely accepted facts to show that none of the alternative theories come close to accounting for these basic details. Interestingly enough, in his massive treatment on the Resurrection, Dr. Michael Licona reduced this list to just the first three facts and demonstrated that the leading alternative theories today still fail to provide explanations that match the evidence the critics themselves are willing to accept.[4]

Conclusion

The Bible gives us clear and compelling eyewitness testimonies that Jesus rose bodily from the dead just as He predicted. God has also left a tremendous amount of corroborating evidence from history, archaeology, and personal experience to show that Jesus indeed rose from the grave.

Skeptics and critics have developed numerous alternative theories in their attempts to overthrow the Resurrection of Jesus Christ. The next section of this book will examine whether these proposals can stand up to scrutiny and account for the evidence.

---

4   Michael R. Licona, *The Resurrection of Jesus*, p. 468.

Section Two:
Alternative Theories

6 Did Someone Else Take the Place of Jesus on the Cross?

As we have seen, if Jesus rose from the dead, then He is precisely who He claimed to be: the Son of God and the only Way to the Father (Matthew 16:16–17; John 14:6). We have also seen that the teaching of the Resurrection was so central to the early church's message that the Christian faith truly stands or falls with the Resurrection. As such, critics and skeptics have relentlessly attacked this event. They have developed scores of alternate theories in their efforts to explain away the facts, since believing God raised Jesus from the dead is unacceptable to them. The most popular of these theories will be examined in forthcoming chapters. The first three of these alternate claims make little effort, if any, to deal with the text of Scripture, the extra-biblical evidence, or the "minimal facts."

Claims from the Qur'an

One of the more popular arguments against the Resurrection of Jesus, particularly in Islamic circles, is derived from the Qur'an, which states the following:

> That they said (in boast), "We killed Christ Jesus the son of Mary, the Messenger of Allah"—but they killed him not, nor crucified him, but so it was made to appear to them, and those who differ therein are full of doubts, with no (certain) knowledge, but only conjecture to follow, for of a surety they killed him not—nay, Allah raised

him up unto Himself; and Allah is Exalted in Power,
Wise. (Qur'an, 4:157–158, Yusuf Ali)[1]

In other words, the Qur'an teaches that Jesus did not even die
on the Cross. Instead, Muslims believe that at or around the time
of His arrest, Jesus was taken to heaven while one of His disciples,
probably Judas, was transformed to look just like Him. So this
disciple was arrested, beaten, and crucified in His place.

There are multiple problems with this statement in the
Qur'an. First, this passage refers to Jews who rejected and claimed
to have crucified "Christ Jesus." Many people today assume that
Christ is part of the name of Jesus, and it seems that Muhammad
believed this too. But *Christ* is actually the Greek word for
Messiah (Hebrew *mashiyach*). So rather than being a first name
(or a last name), *Christ* is a title identifying Jesus as the Jewish
Messiah, and non-Christian Jews would never identify Jesus as
the Messiah. For the sake of argument, even if these Jews did
think of Him that way, they never would have boasted about
crucifying Him, because they would have viewed Him as the one
they had long been waiting for.

Second, these same Jews would not have used the phrase
"messenger of Allah." Allah is not the same as Yahweh, the God of
the Bible, and these Jews did not believe Jesus was "the Messenger
of Allah."

Third, this passage poses a theological problem for Muslims
because it shows Allah as a deceiver who tricked people into
thinking they had crucified Jesus. If Allah is a deceiver, how
could the Qur'an be trusted as being true?

Finally, this passage denies that Jesus died by crucifixion,
yet this is the first of the five minimal facts accepted by the vast
majority of scholars. The biblical writers affirmed Jesus was
crucified, as did several non-Christian writers in the first century
after His death, including the Jewish historian Josephus and the
Roman historian Tacitus. Bear in mind that the Qur'an was not
written until the seventh century AD.

---

[1] Cited by David Wood in "The Irony of the Qur'an—Surah 4:157–158."
Available at < http://www.answeringmuslims.com/2008/07/irony-of-
quransurah-4157-158.html>. Accessed January 16, 2013.

The Gospel of Barnabas

Further support for this case of mistaken identity is also drawn from a book known as the *Gospel of Barnabas* (*GoB*), not to be confused with the *Epistle of Barnabas*, which is a late first century Christian document. According to the *GoB*, Jesus was taken to the third heaven by angels just before the soldiers and Judas arrived to arrest Him and then the following event took place:

> Judas entered impetuously before all into the chamber whence Jesus had been taken up. And the disciples were sleeping. Whereupon the wonderful God acted wonderfully, insomuch that Judas was so changed in speech and in face to be like Jesus that we believed him to be Jesus... And as he was saying this the soldiery entered, and laid their hands upon Judas, because he was in every way like to Jesus. (*Gospel of Barnabas*, 216)

As with the aforementioned claims of the Qur'an, there are several problems with this passage. It is readily apparent that the book is not an ancient document composed by the Apostle Barnabas. Instead, it is a sixteenth century forgery and was drafted to promote Islamic claims about the Bible and Jesus. For example, the book repeatedly attempts to show that Muhammad is superior to Jesus, and it reflects an Islamic understanding of Jesus. Ironically, the introduction of the book states that "the great and wonderful God hath during these past days visited us by his prophet Jesus *Christ* in great mercy..." (emphasis added). Yet in chapter 42 of this forgery, Jesus, echoing lines from John the Baptist in the Bible, specifically denies being the Messiah. Anyone with an elementary understanding of Hebrew and Greek would immediately recognize as a denial of being the Christ, since as mentioned earlier, the terms *Messiah* and *Christ* are synonymous. Indeed it is strange that some Muslim apologists cite the *GoB* since it clearly contradicts the Qur'an. The *GoB* explicitly denies that Jesus is the Messiah (*GoB*, 42), reserving that title for Muhammad (*GoB*, 97), yet the Qur'an calls Jesus the Messiah (Christ) on multiple occasions (e.g., Qur'an 4:171 and 5:75).

There are numerous reasons that show the *Gospel of Barnabas* to be an obvious forgery. Every quotation of the Old and New Testament is from the Latin Vulgate, which was translated by Jerome around AD 400, more than three centuries after Barnabas lived. The *GoB* even includes quotations of the Italian poet Dante (c. 1265–1321). The book contains numerous historical and geographical errors, such as the claim that Jesus sailed on the Sea of Galilee to Nazareth (*GoB*, 20), but Nazareth is about 15 miles away from that sea and cannot be reached via water.

This forgery also states that Jesus was born while Pilate was governor (*GoB*, 3), but Pilate actually became governor around AD 26 or 27, about the time Jesus began His ministry. It refers to Barnabas as one of the original 12 disciples and even has Jesus, during His ministry, address him as Barnabas. But Barnabas was not one of the original 12 disciples. And even if he had been one of them, he would have been known at that time by his birth name, Joseph, since he wasn't nicknamed Barnabas, which means "son of encouragement," until he sold a field and gave the proceeds to the apostles (Acts 4:37).

Conclusion

The mistaken identity view has zero textual support from any early writers and contradicts the first minimal fact—Jesus died by crucifixion. Instead, it is based on writings that were composed no sooner than AD 600. And it requires an act of deception by the god who supposedly performed the miraculous transformation of the disciple to look like Jesus, so the deity who allegedly wrought this miracle would be a deceitful being, and therefore certainly not worthy of anyone's trust.

7 Is the Resurrection of Jesus Just the Stuff of Legend?

In chapter 2, it was mentioned that some skeptics and critics claim that the beliefs about Christ's Resurrection were simply legends that developed over decades as Christianity spread throughout the Roman Empire. This theory does not deny that Jesus ever existed, as the "Christ Myth" view to be examined in the following chapter does. Instead, the legend view typically sees Jesus as an actual person who lived in Israel during the first century AD, but His miracles and other major achievements were simply embellishments made by overzealous followers.

Dan Barker, a former pastor, well-known skeptic, and co president of the Freedom from Religion Foundation, is one of the best-known skeptics to have touted the legend view.

> There have been many reasons for doubting [Jesus rose bodily from the grave], but the consensus among critical scholars today appears to be that the story is a "legend." During the 60–70 years it took for the Gospels to be composed, the original story went through a growth period that began with the unadorned idea that Jesus, like Grandma, had "died and gone to heaven" and ended with a fantastic narrative produced by a later generation of believers that included earthquakes, angels, an eclipse, a resuscitated corpse, and a spectacular bodily ascension into the clouds.

> The earliest Christians believed in the "spiritual" resurrection of Jesus. The story later evolved over time into a "bodily" resurrection.[1]

Barker attempts to support his proposal by listing the number of "Extraordinary Events" described by the various biblical writers in their respective Resurrection narratives—he also throws into the mix the non-canonical and sometimes bizarre work called the Gospel of Peter. He counts the number of events he considers to be extraordinary with a date he assigns to each of the writings and claims that the number of these events increases as time passes, showing that the legend grew as time went on.

There are multiple problems with Barker's claims and the legend view in general. Barker, like other proponents of this view, does not even attempt to account for the evidence described in chapters 2–5. While these people may accept that Jesus died on the Cross, they deny that the disciples, Paul, and James believed that Jesus appeared to them, and they reject the empty tomb. So those who cling to the legend view are at odds with practically all historians, even the critical ones that Barker claims support his view. Let's take a look at some of Barker's specific errors. Here is a chart illustrating his claims.

Dan Barker's List of Extraordinary Events in the Resurrection Accounts

Writer	Barker's Date	Resurrection Passage	Extraordinary Events
Paul	50–55	1 Corinthians 15:3–8	0
Mark	70	Mark 16	1
Matthew	80	Matthew 28	4
Luke	85	Luke 24	5
Peter	85–90	Gospel of Peter fragment	6
John	95	John 20–21	8+

[1] Dan Barker, "Did Jesus Really Rise from the Dead," in Russ Kick, ed., *Abuse Your Illusions: The Disinformation Guide to Media Mirages and Establishment Lies* (New York, NY: The Disinformation Company Ltd, 2003), p. 311.

First, the dates Barker assigns to each of the writings other than 1 Corinthians are highly unlikely. Conservative scholars often assign dates prior to AD 70 for all of these writings except the Gospel of John (c. AD 85) and the Gospel of Peter (late second century). Of course, Barker opts for dates consistent with the critical theologians who have sought to "demythologize" the Scriptures. That is, they try to weed out what they believe to be mythological elements in the Gospels so that they can ascertain "what really happened."

There are excellent reasons for rejecting Barker's dates. For example, Luke wrote his Gospel prior to writing Acts, and there are strong indications that Acts was penned several years before Paul's execution (c. AD 66). The book of Acts closes with Paul under house arrest in Rome enjoying relative freedom to preach, teach, and receive guests (Acts 28:30–31). In all likelihood, he was going to be set free, since according to Festus, "He had committed nothing deserving of death," nor could Festus make any specific charges against Paul (Acts 25:25–26). After hearing Paul's defense, King Agrippa agreed with Festus, stating, "This man might have been set free if he had not appealed to Caesar" (Acts 26:32).

It was during his time of incarceration in Caesarea and Rome that he wrote the "prison epistles" of Ephesians, Colossians, Philippians, and Philemon. These circumstances are far different than the condition Paul describes at the end of 2 Timothy. Here we find Paul abandoned and fully expecting to be executed (2 Timothy 4:6–16). He implores Timothy to hasten his visit and to bring his cloak (v. 13), indicating that Paul did not enjoy the comforts of his own rented home as he did in Acts 28.[2]

Second, even if we grant the unlikely dates used by Barker, his methodology contains serious mistakes. He ignores the various reasons why the authors wrote what they did and presumes that each of the authors attempted to provide an exhaustive

---

[2] For more details about the possibility of Paul's release from his first Roman imprisonment and his subsequent travels, see Donald Guthrie, *New Testament Introduction* (Downers Grove, IL: InterVarsity Press, 1996, 4th revised ed.), pp. 622–624, and John William Drane, *Introducing the New Testament* (Oxford: Lion Publishing, 2000, revised and updated), p. 365.

account of post-Crucifixion events. This is clearly not the case, since in 1 Corinthians 15:3–7 Paul recited an earlier creedal statement dating to within a few years of the Resurrection. Creeds are not meant to provide every detail available. Instead, they are designed to be succinct summaries of essential points. Using Barker's logic, we should conclude that the drafters of the Nicene Creed did not believe that Jesus performed miracles, although they clearly did, but that was not the point of the creed. In 1 Corinthians 15:3–7, Paul specifically mentioned the death, burial, and Resurrection of Jesus before spending much of the chapter explaining the physical, albeit changed, resurrection body. Also, each Gospel writer reported certain details that fit his respective purpose.

Barker engages in some peculiar counting to make the number of extraordinary events line up in the order he desires. For example, he does not count Paul's description of Christ's appearances in 1 Corinthians 15, but he does count such appearances as extraordinary in Luke and John. This is because Barker sets himself up as the one who gets to determine what qualifies as extraordinary. Further, he counts the appearance of two angels described in Luke and John as two separate events, even though the appearance of these angels is clearly one event.

Third, Barker's methodology backfires when we examine other aspects of the accounts to see if there are any signs of legendary development. Consider the amount of eyewitnesses of the risen Christ described in each of these accounts. Mark has an angel telling the women that Jesus was going to appear to the 11 disciples (Mark 11:7). John describes Jesus appearing to no less than 12 people. Matthew reports that Jesus appeared to at least 13 people. Luke mentioned Jesus being seen by at least 15 people. Paul mentions more than 500 eyewitnesses in 1 Corinthians 15.

So, if we were to apply Barker's methodology to the number of eyewitnesses (and use his dates for the sake of argument), then we would have to conclude that the list in 1 Corinthians 15 is by far the most legendary of these works. And since this passage in 1 Corinthians 15 is part of an early creedal statement dating to within five years of Christ's death, we should conclude that each of the Resurrection accounts was written earlier—within five years of the events described.[3] No scholar would accept such early dates, and these books weren't written this early; however, this exercise illustrates the obtuseness of Barker's thinking on the subject.

The legend view fails to make sense of numerous details found in the Scriptures. For example, one of the evidences for the authenticity of the Resurrection accounts is the role played by the women in discovering the empty tomb and being the first witnesses of the risen Savior. If later authors were inventing legendary details to incorporate into the story, they would have never positioned women in such an important role. Josephus, writing at about the same time as the Gospel writers, stated the following concerning the admissibility of women as witnesses: "But let not the testimony of women be admitted, on account of the levity and boldness of their sex."[4] This does not reflect biblical teaching, but was likely taught by the scribes and Pharisees. Wright correctly describes the presence of women in the text.

> We do not know (despite repeated scholarly assertions) exactly when the evangelists first put pen to paper. But we must affirm that the story they tell is one which goes back behind Paul, back to the very early period, before anyone had time to think, "It would be good to tell stories about Jesus rising from the dead; what will best serve our apologetic needs?" It is far, far easier to assume that the women were there at the beginning, just as, three days earlier, they had been there at the end.[5]

Finally, Barker claimed that Christ's earliest followers believed that Jesus merely underwent a "spiritual resurrection" rather than a physical resurrection. This claim is demonstrably false and will be addressed in detail in chapter 11.

---

[3] For an excellent critique of Barker's chapter, see David Wood, "A Response to Dan Barker's 'Did Jesus Really Rise from the Dead?'" in James Patrick Holding, ed., *Defending the Resurrection: Did Jesus Rise from the Dead?* (Longwood, FL: Xulon Press, 2010), pp. 81–95.

[4] Josephus, trans. William Whiston, *Antiquities of the Jews*, 4.219.

[5] N.T. Wright, *The Resurrection of the Son of God* (Minneapolis, MN: Fortress Press, 2003), p. 608.

Conclusion

The legend view provides a great example of how the various alternatives to the Resurrection might be able to account for certain details in the text but fail miserably when compared to all the data. Consequently, proponents of these views tend to pick and choose the verses that can be twisted into their scenarios and ignore all of the details that contradict their views, demonstrating once again that their unbelief in the Resurrection generally stems from their anti-Christian worldview rather than a careful study of known data.

8 Was the Resurrection Copied from Pagan "Saviors"?

In recent years, a thoroughly baseless view has been promoted through a handful of movies and by some of the "new atheists," particularly those who would be classified as "Jesus Mythers" or "Christ Mythers." This copycat proposal is similar to the legend view in that it does not even attempt to account for the historical data. So, many of the critiques of the legend view are relevant here. Essentially, this idea states that Jesus never really lived but was invented by early church leaders who based their ideas about Him on myths of pagan gods from various cultures.

The Mythers' Myth

While popularized in movies like *The God Who Wasn't There*, *Zeitgeist*, and *Religulous*, the copycat view has practically no support among scholars, whether critical or skeptical.[1] "Mythers" often claim that there are no extra-biblical writings about Jesus from the Jews or Romans. For example, the *Zeitgeist* film states:

> Furthermore, is there any non-biblical historical
> evidence of any person, living with the name Jesus,

[1] Gary Habermas cited two atheist scholars who have questioned whether or not Jesus was a real person: G.A. Wells and philosopher Michael Martin. See Gary R. Habermas, *The Historical Jesus*, pp. 27–45. After examining the claims of these men, Habermas stated, "We have seen that these attempts are refuted at almost every turn by the early and eyewitness testimony presented by Paul and others, as well as by the early date of the Gospels" (p. 45).

the Son of Mary, who traveled about with twelve followers, healing people and the like? There are numerous historians who lived in and around the Mediterranean either during or soon after the assumed life of Jesus. How many of these historians document this figure? Not one.

This claim is simply false. Gary Habermas surveyed seventeen ancient historical sources from Jews, Romans, and Gnostics that mention Jesus. Of these seventeen sources, eleven speak of His death with five of these specifically mentioning that He was crucified. Furthermore, seven of the seventeen sources report or imply that Christ's followers claimed He had been raised from the dead.[2] It is no wonder that historians are virtually unanimous in their belief that Jesus of Nazareth truly lived in the first century AD and is the historical figure behind Christianity.

The arguments for the copycat view were earlier promoted by a former Anglican priest and professor of Greek and New Testament at the University of Toronto. In his book *The Pagan Christ*, Tom Harpur garnered his ideas from nineteenth and twentieth century writers Alvin Boyd Kuhn, Godfrey Higgins, and Gerald Massey, who had pushed the idea that virtually all of the main ideas of Christianity and Judaism came from Egyptian religions.

W. Ward Gasque's research on these men sheds light on the type of "scholarship" we are dealing with here. Consider the fact that Harpur identified Kuhn as an "Egyptologist" who is "one of the single greatest geniuses of the twentieth century" and a man who "towers above all others of recent memory in intellect and his understanding of the world's religions." In reality, Kuhn was a high school language teacher, and neither Kuhn, Higgins, nor Massey appears in *Who Was Who in Egyptology* or in Pratt's exhaustive bibliography on ancient Egypt. Dr. Gasque contacted twenty leading Egyptologists and asked them about Kuhn, Higgins, Massey, and their claims. Of the ten scholars who responded, only one had even heard of these men, while all of them rejected their assertions. Gasque concluded, "If one were able to survey the members of the major learned societies dealing with antiquity, it would be difficult to find more than a

[2]   Ibid., pp. 224–225.

handful who believe that Jesus of Nazareth did not walk the dusty roads of Palestine in the first three decades of the Common Era. Evidence for Jesus as a historical personage is incontrovertible."[3] Simply put, these men are not in any way recognized as experts on ancient Egypt, yet their ideas are being promoted by atheists who are intent on pushing the copycat Messiah myth.

If true, these claims would deal a significant blow to the Christian faith as they would call into serious question the historicity of the life and ministry of Jesus. More importantly, at least as far as this study is concerned, if early Christians simply copied their ideas about the Crucifixion and Resurrection of Jesus from pagan beliefs, then the gospel message would be undermined and we would still be in our sins. Nevertheless, there simply is no warrant for the copycat scenarios.

Pagan Saviors?

There is no shortage of misinformation from Mythers on this subject. An entire book could be written to counter the false teachings that compare Jesus to other ancient figures. These so-called "saviors" were rarely, if ever, considered to be saviors, although many were considered at some point to be gods, while others were thought to have been miracle workers or magicians. Let's examine one of these individuals to see if there is any merit in the assertions of the *Zeitgeist* film. There is little need to offer an additional critique of *Religulous* since Bill Maher simply copied his claims from *Zeitgeist*. Furthermore, examining all of the claims would become incredibly redundant since many of the assertions are regurgitated for each "savior" figure.

The following claims are made about the Egyptian god Horus in *Zeitgeist*:

- He was born of a virgin called Isis Meri (Mary?) on December 25th.
- His birth was marked by a star in the east.
- He was adored as an infant by three kings.

[3] Cited in W. Ward Gasque, "The Leading Religion Writer in Canada ... Does He Know What He's Talking About?" Available at <www.hnn.us/articles/6641.html> Accessed October 27, 2012.

- He was a teacher by age 12.
- He was baptized by "Anup the Baptizer" who was subsequently decapitated.
- Horus started his ministry at age 30.
- He had 12 disciples and performed miracles.
- He was known as the "Lamb of God" and "the Light."
- He was crucified and lay dead for three days before being resurrected.

Is there any solid evidence for these claims? Absolutely not! In fact, there are good reasons to reject every single point either because it is patently false or because, in many cases even if the claim were true, it would not impact Christianity in any way because the idea is not even found in Scripture.

First, there is no record of Horus being born on December 25th. Instead, the only reference that gives a date for his birth places it on day 31 of Khoiak, which roughly corresponds to our month of November. Even if Horus was born on December 25th, this would be irrelevant since the Bible never says that this is the date of the birth of Christ.[4]

Second, no ancient record exists where Isis is called Mary, nor is she ever portrayed as a virgin at the time of the birth of Horus. There is no record of a star rising in the east at his birth, nor do any ancient records show him being admired by three kings. Once again we see a listing of irrelevant details, which shows that the originators of these false connections to Horus have not carefully read the Bible. Even if three kings did visit the infant Horus, it would be irrelevant. The Bible states that magi, not kings, visited Jesus a while after His birth, and it does not tell us how many made the journey.[5]

Third, no Egyptian records mention Horus being a teacher at age 12, and there certainly is no record of anyone named Anup the Baptizer who later lost his head. In fact, there is never any

---

[4] For more information on whether or not Jesus was born on December 25th, see Tim Chaffey, "More Christmas Misconceptions—Part Two" at <http:// midwestapologetics.org/blog/?p=267>.

[5] For more details about the magi and the timing of their visit, see Tim Chaffey, "We Three Kings" at < http://www.answersingenesis.org/articles/2010/12/14/we-three-kings>. Accessed October 27, 2012.

mention of baptism for Horus. While he did have some followers, there is no indication that he had a select group of 12.

Fourth, Horus was never called "Lamb of God" or "the Light." However, he did have some titles, such as Great God, Chief of the Powers, Master of Heaven, and Avenger of His Father.[6]

Finally, Horus certainly was not crucified. This would have been difficult since the first writings about him are from well over a thousand years before crucifixion was even invented. Just as he was not crucified, Horus certainly was never resurrected from the dead as Jesus was.

Mythers have raised similar arguments about many other gods or "saviors," including Mithra, Zoroaster, Buddha, Krishna, Osiris, Dionysus, and Attus. Yet despite their best efforts, the ancient records of these individuals have very little in common with Jesus, and in some cases, the few similarities in details only arose after the influence of Christian missionaries.

The fact is that the Christian belief in the Resurrection of Jesus did not borrow from any group of people, and there exists a strong agreement among historians that the pagan mystery religions had minimal influence in first century Israel.[7] In many of these "copycat" claims, the common pagan belief regarding an annual dying and rising god symbolizing the changing seasons is absurdly touted as a parallel to the *physical* death and *physical* Resurrection of Jesus. In his voluminous work on the Resurrection, N.T. Wright examined the dying and rising god cults of antiquity and concluded, "Did any worshipper in these cults, from Egypt to Norway, at any time in antiquity, think that actual human beings, having died, actually came back to life? Of course not." As Wright sarcastically noted, "When Paul preached in Athens, nobody said, 'Ah, yes, a new version of Osiris and such like.'"[8]

---

[6] J.P. Holding, "Pagan Christ, Egyptian Front: Horus, Osiris," in J.P. Holding, ed., *Shattering the Christ Myth: Did Jesus Not Exist?* (Longview, FL: Xulon Press, 2008), p. 224.

[7] Grant expressed the opinion of many scholars when he stated, "Judaism was a milieu to which doctrines of the deaths and rebirths of mythical gods seems so entirely foreign that the emergence of such a fabrication from its midst is very hard to credit." Michael Grant, *Jesus: An Historian's Review of the Gospels* (New York: Scribner's, 1977), p. 199.

[8] Wright, *Resurrection*, pp. 80–81.

Was the Resurrection "All Greek" to the Disciples?

The biblical view of the Resurrection did not borrow from the Greeks. The notion of bodily resurrection was abhorrent to these people since they viewed the material world as evil. As such, why would anyone desire to undergo physical resurrection? This is one of the reasons Paul spent so much time explaining to the Corinthians the physical nature of the general resurrection (1 Corinthians 15).

A unique study of ancient Greco-Roman literature about the dead has provided further evidence that early Christians did not copy the idea of the Resurrection from the ancient world. Deborah Thompson Prince surveyed ancient writings about appearances of the dead and was able to categorize these stories into four classes: disembodied spirits, revenants,[9] heroes, and translated mortals.[10] Her findings are devastating to the copycat theory since the resurrected Jesus described in Scripture does not match any of them. This should have been expected by any serious researcher, but what is truly interesting is that Luke seems to combine elements and precise phrases from stories of all four classes to show that Jesus surpassed each of these ideas. This leads Prince to conclude the following:

> I submit that the method at work in Lk. 24 is an attempt to disorient the reader in order to reconfigure the traditions known to the author and reader in light of the disciples' extraordinary experience of the resurrected Jesus. After all, Luke can only describe Jesus' post-resurrection appearances with the vocabulary and literary models he has at his disposal. But what if these are deemed inadequate for his purpose, and no one type of apparition is thought sufficient to represent what the disciples had experienced? In this case Luke would be left with insufficient language and models. If, however, all possible models are incorporated, thereby displaying the breadth and magnitude of Jesus' resurrected presence, while at the same time

---

[9] A revenant is a person or ghost who has returned from the dead.

[10] Deborah Thompson Prince, "The 'Ghost' of Jesus: Luke 24 in Light of Ancient Narratives of Post-Mortem Apparitions," *Journal for the Study of the New Testament* 29:3 (2007): 287–301.

the limitations of each model are highlighted, then the author is able to work within the parameters of the literary and cultural expectations of the audience to express a phenomenon that surpasses those expectations.[11]

Wright devoted more than 50 pages to examining "the range of options for belief about the dead that were available in the classical world of late antiquity—roughly two or three hundred years either side of the time of Jesus." He conclusively demonstrated that the Christian doctrine on Christ's Resurrection did not borrow from other beliefs.[12]

Was the Resurrection Copied from Jewish Beliefs?

Finally, the Christian belief in Christ's Resurrection did not really even borrow from popular Jewish beliefs of the day, although this would have been the natural place to start. First century Jews, except for the Sadducees, generally believed in a future bodily resurrection of all people. The Old Testament prophet Daniel wrote, "And many of those who sleep in the dust of the earth shall awake, some to everlasting life, some to shame and everlasting contempt" (Daniel 12:2). This view was reflected in Martha's response to Jesus before He raised her brother Lazarus back to life. He told her that Lazarus would live again. Martha stated, "I know that he will rise again in the resurrection at the last day" (John 11:24). In Revelation 20, John reaffirmed and expanded upon the concept of a future resurrection of all the dead.

The Christian belief did actually stem from Jewish writings. The Old Testament does contain prophecies concerning the Resurrection of the Messiah (Psalm 16:10; Isaiah 53:8–12), but the Jews did not properly understand the details of these passages. Also, some of the teachings about the Messiah implied the Resurrection, such as the idea that He would have an eternal priesthood (Psalm 110:4; cf. Hebrews 7:25) and that He would physically return to the earth (Zechariah 12:10, 14:4; cf. Acts 1:11).

So, the early church did not copy the popular beliefs of first century Jews on the Resurrection. However, Jesus did fulfill the various prophecies that implied the Messiah would rise again.

---

[11] Ibid., p. 297.
[12] Wright, *Resurrection*, pp. 38–39.

Conclusion

So far, we have looked at three of the skeptical attempts to explain away the Resurrection of Jesus. We have seen that each of these positions in their various forms fail miserably in accounting for the details surrounding the Lord's conquering of death. For the most part, these three views do not even attempt to interact with the New Testament and other historical data. Instead, their proponents have made outlandish claims without any supporting evidence. And yet, it is often these same proponents who accuse Christians of having blind faith.

Ironically, it is the skeptic who blindly trusts in wild assertions to escape the one thing their belief system fears most: the risen Lord and Savior Jesus Christ. Sadly, instead of humbling themselves and being reconciled to God through faith in Christ, these skeptics mock their Creator and the only means of salvation. If you are one of these skeptics, I urge you to stop trying to justify your unbelief by clinging to these bizarre and unsubstantiated beliefs, repent of your sins, and call upon the risen Lord to save you from your sins.

9 Did the Disciples Experience Mass Hallucinations?

One of the infallible proofs of Christ's Resurrection is the fact that He repeatedly appeared to people after being crucified. As previously demonstrated, the vast majority of historians accept as fact that the disciples believed Jesus had appeared to them, which led to their bold proclamations that He had risen from the dead. Within the biblical worldview, the obvious explanation for these appearances is exactly what the Bible states—Jesus died, was buried, and then rose again (1 Corinthians 15:3–8). However, this conclusion does not sit well with liberal theologians and other skeptics and critics because of the obvious implications. That is, if Jesus rose from the dead as He predicted He would, then this event would confirm His teachings, and this is unacceptable for those who do not want to trust in Christ.[1]

---

[1]   A rare exception is found in the work of Orthodox Jewish writer Pinchas Lapide, who believed the evidence was so strong for the Resurrection that he wrote, "In regard to the future resurrection of the dead, I am and remain a Pharisee. Concerning the resurrection of Jesus on Easter Sunday, I was for decades a Sadducee. I am no longer a Sadducee." Pinchas Lapide, *The Resurrection of Jesus: A Jewish Perspective* (Minneapolis, MN: Augsburg Fortress, 1983), p. 125. He even criticized professing Christians who denied the Resurrection stating, "I cannot rid myself of the impression that some modern Christian theologians are ashamed of the material fact of the resurrection. Their varying attempts at dehistoricizing the Easter experience which give the lie to all four evangelists are simply not understandable in any other way." Ibid., p. 130. Sadly, Lapide did not convert to Christianity.

Hallucinations

Throughout history some individuals have experienced hallucinations, meaning that they have perceived someone or something to be present even though that person or thing was not objectively there. Hallucinations are common among certain types of drug users and among those who are grieving the loss of a loved one. The disciples were certainly grieving over the death of Christ, so critical theologians have argued that the disciples may have simply experienced hallucinations of Jesus, causing them to conclude that He had risen from the dead. This theory, or some variation of it, has actually been proposed by numerous critical scholars and currently is their leading alternate explanation to the Resurrection.

Michael Goulder (1927–2010) was a liberal biblical scholar who refers to Peter's devastated psychological and emotional state after Jesus was crucified as the basis for a grief-induced hallucination. He then told the other disciples about this event and they shared in a group delusion, similar to some of the purported sightings of Mary or UFOs.[2]

Atheist Gerd Lüdemann (b. 1946) has promoted a similar idea. He argues that Peter, after experiencing a hallucination of Jesus stemming from his mental torment, informed the other disciples, who subsequently shared a group hallucination. Lüdemann's bias against supernatural activity is a driving force in his interpretation of the data. He stated that it is nonsensical to believe that Jesus rose physically from the dead because one would have to believe that a decaying corpse, already cold and without blood in its brain, could be made alive again.[3]

Although it is true that many grief-stricken people are prone to hallucinate, there are multiple problems with these explanations regarding the appearances of Jesus. Concerning hallucinations today, only a small percentage can be described as vivid, and they are more common among women and the elderly.

---

[2] Michael Goulder, "Baseless Fabric of a Vision," in Gavin D'Costa, ed., *Resurrection Reconsidered* (Oxford: Oneworld, 1996), p. 53.

[3] Gerd Lüdemann, "Opening Statement," in Paul Copan and Ronald Tacelli, eds. *Jesus' Resurrection: Fact or Figment?* (Downers Grove, IL: InterVarsity Press, 2000), p. 45.

Additionally, there is essentially no support for the idea of a group hallucination.[4] Yet these critics propose that a large group of younger men had a shared vivid hallucination of Jesus.

Henry Morris correctly pointed out some of the absurdities of this position.

> Such hallucinations, if this is what they were, are quite unique and should warrant careful psychological scrutiny. These [supposed hallucinations of the disciples] were experienced by a considerable number of different individuals, all seeing the same vision, but in different groups, at different times, both indoors and outdoors, on a hilltop, along a roadway, by a lakeshore, and other places. Furthermore, they were not looking for Jesus at all. Several times they didn't recognize Him at first, and at least once actually believed it was a ghost until He convinced them otherwise. He invited them to touch Him and they recognized the wounds in His hands (John 20:27; Luke 24:39). They watched Him eat with them (Luke 24:41–43). On one occasion, over 500 different people saw Him at one time (1 Corinthians 15:6), most of whom were still living at the time when the evidence was being used.[5]

Still more problems exist for this popular skeptical view. How does one explain the appearance of Jesus to Paul on the road to Damascus? Surely Paul was not grieving over the death of Jesus. He was zealously persecuting followers of Christ and "still breathing threats and murder against the disciples" (Acts 9:1). He was not in any state of mind to experience a hallucination of Jesus, particularly one that would transform his life so drastically. Yet Paul's experience is one of the five minimal facts, meaning it is well-evidenced and accepted by the vast majority of scholars on the subject.

Also among these key evidences are the empty tomb and the conversion of James due to a purported post-Resurrection

---

[4] Michael R. Licona, *The Resurrection of Jesus*, pp. 483–484.
[5] Henry Morris, *Many Infallible Proofs* (Green Forest, AR: Master Books, 1996), p. 103.

appearance of Jesus. The mass hallucination theory cannot account for the empty tomb without appealing to another highly improbable theory, such as the reburial or stolen body views we will examine in chapters 12 and 13. Nor can the hallucination view make sense of the conversion of James. While James may have grieved the loss of his half-brother, the death of Jesus would have confirmed his skeptical view of Christ's claim to be the Savior. James likely came to believe in Jesus as the Jewish Messiah upon seeing the risen Lord.[6]

Even the non-Christian Pinchas Lapide rejected the hallucination theory. After examining the various claims he wrote, "If the defeated and depressed group of disciples overnight could change into a victorious movement of faith, based only on autosuggestion or self-deception—without a fundamental faith experience—then this would be a much greater miracle than the resurrection itself."[7]

Lapide is correct. So, the famous anti-miraculous dictum of David Hume (the eighteenth-century skeptical philosopher) can be turned around on the skeptics. Hume argued that the wise man "proportions his belief to the evidence,"[8] so he thought the evidence would always favor a naturalistic explanation over a supernatural one. Yet in this case, it would be a far greater miracle for entire groups of people in different mental states to undergo shared hallucinations on different occasions, in different places, and for different reasons.

The skeptic may claim that any naturalistic explanation, no matter how absurd, always trumps a supernatural explanation, yet this reveals more about the person's anti-supernatural bias

---

[6] As explained in chapter 3, Scripture does not explicitly state that James converted upon seeing Christ. However, most scholars agree that his conversion occurred when he saw the risen Savior (or, from the critical viewpoint, when he believed he was witnessing the risen Christ). The Bible reveals that James rejected Christ's claims prior to the Crucifixion (John 7:5), and just several weeks after Jesus died, James is counted among the believers in the upper room (Acts 1:14). What happened between these two events? Paul told the Corinthians that Jesus appeared to James alive and well after being killed and buried (1 Corinthians 15:7).

[7] Pinchas Lapide, *The Resurrection of Jesus: A Jewish Perspective*, p. 126.

[8] David Hume, *An Enquiry concerning Human Understanding* (Oxford, 2nd edition, 1902 reprint of 1777 posthumous edition), § 87.

than it does the evidence. Regarding the Resurrection of Jesus, there is strong historical evidence that Jesus died and was seen alive again. Also, there are no known examples of mass hallucinations, yet some of the eyewitnesses of the risen Savior had already seen at least three people raised from the dead (Luke 7:11–15, 8:49–56; John 11:37–44). Hume's assertion also ignores the fact that millions of people throughout history have claimed to have witnessed a miracle.[9] Furthermore, Geisler showed that it is disingenuous at best to attempt to define miracles out of existence without even examining the evidence for or against them. Hume's argument actually proves too much, for if we were to follow it then we must reject the occurrence of any and every rare event.[10]

Conclusion

Although it is quite popular with critics of the Bible, the mass hallucination view fails at every point. While it may possibly account for some of the post-Resurrection appearances in the mind of the critic, it cannot explain many of the details of these encounters. Also, adherents to this position must rely upon an extremely implausible scenario to explain the empty tomb (see chapters 12 and 13) and to account for the conversions of James and Paul. Finally, mass hallucinations are without precedent while those who traveled with Jesus saw Him bring at least three people back to life, and He predicted His own Resurrection several times. So not only was there precedent for such a miracle, but Jesus repeatedly demonstrated His power over death during His ministry and once again when He gloriously rose from the tomb.

[9] Craig S. Keener, *Miracles: The Credibility of the New Testament Accounts*, volume 1 (Grand Rapids, MI: Baker Academic, 2011), p. 2.
[10] Norman L. Geisler, *Miracles and the Modern Mind: A Defense of Biblical Miracles* (Grand Rapids, MI: Baker, 1992), p. 30.

10 Did the Disciples See Visions Instead of the Risen Lord?

The previous chapter examined the most popular view of the Resurrection held by critics today. The notion that the disciples experienced mass hallucinations was developed to explain away one of the strongest evidences for the Resurrection: the post-Resurrection appearances of the risen Jesus to numerous people over a 40-day period. The view falls short in many respects, but a similar view exists that must be critiqued. Rather than experiencing hallucinations of Jesus, some critics have claimed that the disciples had visions of the Savior.

There are two strands of this view: the naturalistic and the supernatural. In many respects, the naturalistic vision hypothesis is similar to the mass hallucination view and suffers from many of the same flaws.

The supernatural vision hypothesis is different in that it still accepts a miraculous explanation for the events. Essentially, this view states that Jesus spiritually ascended into heaven, leaving His body in the tomb. From heaven Jesus used something akin to mental telepathy to transmit images of Himself to His disciples on earth. These visions were so vivid that the disciples assumed they were actually seeing the resurrected body of Jesus. This position has also been called the telegram or telegraph theory.[1]

---

[1] John Ankerberg and John Weldon, *Handbook of Biblical Evidences* (Eugene, OR: Harvest House, 1997), p. 113. There may be other explanations as to how or why the disciples experienced these visions, but these alternative views encounter the same problems as the one described here.

As with each of these alternative views, the claim that the disciples mistook visions of Jesus for a bodily resurrection is seriously flawed. However, it does a better job of dealing with the historical facts than most of these views, so portions of this view are plausible. For example, several early Christians actually did experience supernatural visions: Stephen (Acts 7:55–56), Peter (Acts 10), Paul (Acts 16:9; 18:9), and John (virtually the whole book of Revelation). But can these types of visions really be confused with the physical appearances described in the Gospels and Acts 1? Not at all!

Additionally, the vision hypothesis cannot account for many of the historical facts. It does not adequately explain the handful of group appearances. By their very nature, visions are individualized incidents, so they are not shared experiences. Yet the Bible records that Jesus appeared to groups of people on several occasions (Luke 24:36; John 20:26–29, 21:1), including an appearance to more than 500 people at one time (1 Corinthians 15:6).

A distinction must be made between objective visions and subjective visions.[2] An objective vision occurs when the natural senses are not employed, but the object being "seen" is real and not imaginary. Stephen's experience of seeing Jesus at the right hand of God may be an example of an objective vision. If someone claims that the disciples had objective visions of Jesus, then they would be admitting that Jesus rose from the dead since the object being seen is real. Consequently, the objective vision is unacceptable to skeptics.

A subjective vision is a specific type of dream or hallucination that often has a religious subject. Nevertheless, it is still simply "a product of our minds and has no cause or reality outside of our mind."[3] As such, the subjective vision hypothesis has the same problems as the hallucination proposals previously mentioned.

Furthermore, the vision hypothesis (whether objective or subjective) does not account for the empty tomb, so adherents to this position must rely upon other untenable positions that claim

---

[2] Gary Habermas and Michael Licona, *The Case for the Resurrection of Jesus* (Grand Rapids, MI: Kregel Publications, 2004), pp. 111–112.
[3] Ibid., p. 112.

someone moved Christ's body or that everyone went to the wrong tomb (these views will be examined in chapters 12 and 13). Adding these untenable positions to the mix does not strengthen this position in any way. Instead, it substantially weakens the case.

Finally, this view does not adequately address the conversions of James and Paul. For example, proponents of this position often claim that Paul had a vision of Jesus on the road to Damascus. However, this account tells us that Paul's traveling companions saw a light (Acts 22:9) and heard a voice (Acts 9:7).

Skeptics have claimed that contradictions exist in Paul's retellings of these events. But the apparent contradiction in Paul's three conversion accounts in Acts 9, 22, and 26 are easily explained. Acts 9:7 states that Paul's companions heard a voice but didn't see anyone. Acts 22:9 reveals that Paul's companions did not "hear the voice of Him who spoke" to Paul. The word translated as "hear" (Greek, akouō) is used by Luke 153 times. Most of the time it refers to hearing, but in over a third of its occurrences (57 times), it refers to listening with the intent to understand. [4] As a modern day example, many women know that their husband or children can *hear* their voice but not really be *listening*. So Paul's companions heard a voice but they did not understand what was being said.

Visions, like dreams and hallucinations, are not shared experiences. Yes, multiple people can have visions and dreams, but they do not share in the same experience. Two people can have similar dreams on the same night, and they might even dream that the other person is in their dream, but the dream was not a shared experience. Upon waking up, the first person could not rightly say to the other, "Remember that conversation we had in that dream?" The second person would have no recollection of the conversation because it took place in the other person's dream.

Paul's encounter with the risen Christ cannot be explained away by appealing to the vision hypothesis. It is true that Paul told King Agrippa that he was not "disobedient to the heavenly vision" (Acts 26:19). However, this should not be taken as evidence that Paul did not believe he had actually seen the

[4] Licona, *The Resurrection of Jesus*, pp. 387–388.

resurrected Savior. First Corinthians 15 makes it clear that Paul believed in the bodily Resurrection of Christ, and that he had seen the Savior. In addition, Luke recorded Paul's speech to Agrippa, and he also firmly believed in the bodily Resurrection. Elsewhere Luke described the tomb as being empty save grave clothes (Luke 24:3, 12), that Jesus claimed to have "flesh and bones" (Luke 24:39), and that Christ's body did not see decay in the grave (Acts 2:27, 31).[5]

Examining an Alleged Modern Example of Mass Visions

In response to the Christian assertion that no examples of mass hallucinations or visions can be found, some skeptics have claimed to have found a case where this has supposedly taken place. Beginning in 1990 and running through 1998, Nancy Fowler claimed to experience visions of Mary on the thirteenth day of each month. Huge crowds soon flocked to Conyers, Georgia to hear the message that Fowler supposedly received. Some of the gatherings were estimated to have attracted over 100,000 visitors.

During these encounters, some people in the crowd claimed to have witnessed miracles, such as the sun spinning or the air smelling of roses. Are these reported events examples of mass hallucination? Can they provide evidence that perhaps the disciples merely underwent a similar experience rather than actually seeing the risen Lord? Not at all! There are major differences between the post-Resurrection appearances of Jesus to His disciples and the alleged miracles in Conyers, Georgia.

First, some skeptics have argued that multiple people claimed to have seen Mary during these gatherings, but this is not what is reported. Nancy Fowler was supposedly having visions of Mary and receiving messages from her. She would then relay those messages to the crowd.

Second, those who gathered at Conyers, Georgia traveled there with the express intent to witness something supernatural

---

[5] Licona examined every use of the Greek word translated as "vision" in Luke's and Paul's writings and showed that there is much ambiguity in the use of this word, so it would be unwise to use it in an attempt to support the vision hypothesis. Licona, *The Resurrection of Jesus*, pp. 329–333.

or to hear a message from someone claiming to have had a vision of Mary. Tens of thousands of people in one place expecting to experience something miraculous undoubtedly worked up a religious fervor in the audience. They were in just the right mental state to deceive themselves into thinking they saw miracles. This is vastly different than the situations in which Christ's disciples claimed to have seen Him. They were not expecting the bodily Resurrection of Jesus, and they did not believe when they were told by someone else that He had been raised. It was only when they saw for themselves the risen Lord and the physical evidence that He had risen (e.g., touched Him and ate with Him) that they believed.

Consider also the alleged miracle of the sun spinning or dancing associated with the supposed apparitions of Mary. This type of "miracle" is a common claim of participants of other alleged Marian apparitions, such as those at Fatima, Portugal, and Medjugorje, Bosnia and Herzegovina. But staring at the sun without a filter for any length of time is dangerous and causes the viewer to see spots and distorts colors. It seems likely that certain attendees experienced these side effects of staring at the sun, and when combined with the religious fervor of the moment they claimed they were witnessing a miracle. This would have the psychological effect of encouraging others to want to see the same thing.[6]

Video footage also exists from one of the gatherings in Conyers of what appears to be hundreds of rose petals carried in the wind during one of the alleged visions. If these were truly rose petals, then they were not mass visions or hallucinations of spectators, and they would account for the smell of roses reported by witnesses. Nor is it difficult to conceive of a non-miraculous cause for hundreds of rose petals in the air at just the right time— someone could have released them into the wind.

---

[6] Another explanation put forth by some Christians is that these alleged miracles were counterfeited by our enemy Satan as a way of distracting people from learning the Gospel. The messages of the so-called apparitions of Mary frequently call attention to "herself" rather than to Jesus Christ. If these were truly appearances of Mary, why wouldn't she encourage people to listen to her Son as she did in John 2:5?

These alleged visions and sightings in Conyers are highly questionable and do not really qualify as a mass vision or mass hallucination. Again, they simply do not compare to the post-Resurrection appearances of Jesus. In these cases, Jesus often appeared when they did not expect Him. He ate and drank with the disciples. He allowed them to touch Him, and they walked with Him and talked with Him. He performed a miracle that could be verified (the catch of 153 large fish). These appearances took place in a variety of places, at different times, and in different settings. Allegedly seeing the sun spin or smelling rose petals just does not compare in any way to seeing, hearing, and touching a person that you have known for years alive again.

Conclusion

Although better in many respects than the other skeptical and critical positions attempting to deal with the historical data, the vision theories cannot account for all of the minimal facts. They cannot properly account for the conversions of Paul and James, nor do they have an adequate explanation for the empty tomb. Hence, they must depend upon one of the improbable scenarios involving the moving of Christ's body.

It is quite clear why skeptics will believe the most absurd ideas to explain away the Resurrection—they refuse to accept any supernatural events, particularly the one in which the Son of God conquers death. This single event smashes their entire naturalistic worldview.

It is less clear why critical scholars are so reluctant to accept the plain words of Scripture on this subject. After all, these people often claim to be Christians, so their rejection of the Resurrection does not stem from an atheistic worldview. Yet the critics have still adopted an anti-biblical worldview and hold to more of a deistic view where God does not miraculously intervene in His creation. No matter what their reasons are for doing so, by rejecting the physical Resurrection of Christ, these critics have denied the heart of the gospel message, showing that they are not true Christians (Romans 10:9; 1 Corinthians 15:3–4, 12–19).

For both the skeptic and the critic the solution is the same. They must repent of their sins and place their faith in the resurrected Lord and Savior Jesus Christ. While they may fear that this would be akin to committing intellectual suicide, we have seen the opposite is true. The bodily Resurrection of Jesus is corroborated by a wealth of demonstrably reliable historical facts and is taught in the eyewitness accounts in God's infallible Word. To reject such a well-evidenced historical event is an anti-intellectual move and reveals a greater problem—an unwillingness to humble oneself before the Creator who sent His Son to die in our place and raised Him from the dead. Jesus paid the penalty for our sins so that we can live eternally with Him. To continue in the rebellion started by our first parents in the Garden of Eden is not only foolish, it is worse than intellectual suicide because the person who refuses the Savior's sacrificial death consigns himself to a miserable, Christ-less eternity in the lake of fire (Revelation 20:11–15).

If you are an unbeliever, I urge you to continue studying the Resurrection of Jesus and call upon the risen Savior for salvation. If you are a believer, please continue to pray for your unsaved friends and family members. If God can save one of the church's greatest persecutors, Saul of Tarsus, and transform him into the Apostle Paul, then He certainly has the ability to reach your lost loved ones with the saving message of the gospel.

11 Did Jesus Rise Physically or Only Spiritually?

As mentioned in chapter 7, Dan Barker claimed that the earliest followers of Jesus believed that Christ only rose spiritually. Of course, as an atheist, Barker does not believe in a spiritual resurrection since that would still mean something supernatural took place.

Devout skeptics are not the only people who try to use the concept of a spiritual resurrection when discussing this topic. Beginning with Origen (AD 185–254), some non-orthodox thinkers have promoted similar ideas. For example, Origen wrote, "Accordingly, it at one time puts off one body which was necessary before, but which is no longer adequate in its changed state, and it exchanges it for a second."[1] Origen did not believe this second body was visible or material but spiritual and ethereal.

What is meant by a spiritual resurrection, and how does it differ from the biblical view? Some liberal theologians have used the concept of a spiritual resurrection to sidestep the issue of the Resurrection. For John Dominic Crossan, it doesn't matter what happened to the body of Jesus once taken down from the Cross. What matters is the meaning that was attached to the concept of resurrection in the early church—that God's "Great Clean-Up" had started to transform this wicked world into one marked by justice, peace, purity, and holiness.[2]

---

[1] Origen, *De Principiis* 7.32, in Philip Schaff, *Ante-Nicene Fathers*, p. 623.
[2] Crossan in Robert B. Stewart, ed., *The Resurrection of Jesus: John Dominic Crossan and N.T. Wright in Dialogue* (Minneapolis, MN: Augsburg Fortress, 2006), p. 25–26.

The Debate Within Evangelicalism

There are some who hold to a different type of spiritual resurrection and are much closer to orthodox thinking in other areas. While affirming that the tomb became empty via miraculous means, some theologians within evangelicalism argue that the body of Jesus vanished and He received a new "body" altogether.

In his book, *I Believe in the Resurrection of Jesus*, George Eldon Ladd (1911–1982) asked the question, "What would an observer have seen if he had stood inside the tomb watching the dead body of Jesus?" Ladd's response perfectly describes a "spiritual resurrection." Ladd stated, "All he would have seen was the sudden and inexplicable disappearance of the body of Jesus."[3] Regarding the post-Resurrection appearances, Ladd claimed "they were momentary appearances of the invisible, risen Lord to the physical sight and senses of the disciples."[4]

The debate on this topic within Evangelicalism came to the forefront in the early 1990s. Murray Harris of Trinity Evangelical Divinity School promoted the concept of a spiritual resurrection in his book, *Raised Immortal*. Harris argued that Christ's resurrected body was more like that of an angel that could materialize at will, but that its normal mode of operation was that of immateriality. Although He affirmed that Jesus rose from the dead (spiritually), He stated that the Resurrection was not genuinely historical:

> But it is not "historical" in the sense of being an incident that was observed by witnesses or even an incident that could have been observed by mortal gaze. We have already noted that there were no witnesses of the Resurrection itself and that in his resurrected state Jesus was not normally visible to the human eye.[5]

In response to these teachings and others like them, Norman Geisler published *The Battle for the Resurrection* in 1989,

---

[3] George Eldon Ladd, *I Believe in the Resurrection of Jesus* (Grand Rapids, MI: Eerdmans, 1975), p. 100.

[4] Ibid.

[5] Murray Harris, *Raised Immortal: Resurrection and Immortality in the New Testament* (Grand Rapids, MI: Eerdmans, 1985), p. 58.

in which a nine-page section and approximately another ten pages throughout discussed the position of Harris. In 1990, Harris published *From Grave to Glory*, which included 130 pages aimed at Geisler's critique. Over the following year, the *Journal of the Evangelical Theological Society* ran several articles and reviews to address the controversy.[6]

While the heat of this debate has died down, the importance of the topic is just as relevant as ever. For those unfamiliar with the issue, this position may not sound all that different than what they have been taught; however, there are some huge distinctions between this view and what the Bible teaches. These distinctions are not just trivial differences either; they impact major areas of doctrine.

Geisler pointed out that the unorthodox views of Christ's resurrected body share three common errors. 1) They deny the materiality of the Resurrection, meaning that they do not believe that Jesus had a real, physical (material) body after the grave. Instead, He is now a spiritual Being who manifested in a body to appear to His disciples. 2) They deny the numerical identity of Christ's resurrected body. This means that they do not believe He was raised in the same body that was placed in the tomb. 3) They deny the historicity of the Resurrection, teaching instead that it did not occur in our observable space and time. "In other words, the resurrection body cannot be observed as part of the empirical world; it is part of salvation history, but not by nature a part of regular, observable history."[7]

What Does the Bible Teach about Christ's Resurrection Body?

There are several relevant passages to consider when answering this question. Jesus talked about the nature of His resurrected body both before and after His Resurrection. Early in His ministry,

---

[6] The *JETS* articles included an overview of the conflict by Francis J. Beckwith, a brief review of the two positions by Gary Habermas, and a rather scathing review of Geisler's work by Scot McKnight. Geisler was given an opportunity to respond the following year.

[7] Norman L. Geisler, *The Battle for the Resurrection* (Nashville, TN: Thomas Nelson, 1988), pp. 105–106.

Jesus cleansed the temple for the first time.[8] As He drove the people out, the following exchange took place.

> So the Jews answered and said to Him, "What sign do You show to us, since You do these things?" Jesus answered and said to them, "Destroy this temple, and in three days I will raise it up." Then the Jews said, "It has taken forty-six years to build this temple, and will You raise it up in three days?" But He was speaking of the temple of His body. (John 2:18–21)

This passage was mentioned in chapter 2 since in it Jesus predicted His own Resurrection. But He also taught an important point about the nature of His Resurrected body: "Destroy *this temple*, and in three days I will raise *it* up . . . But He was speaking of the temple of *His body*" (emphasis added). So it was His body that would be destroyed (killed), but it would also be that same body that would be raised up. Those who argue that Jesus received a different "body" at His Resurrection contradict the Lord's specific statement here.

After rising from the dead, the materiality of Christ's resurrected body was demonstrated on several occasions. Mary Magdalene apparently clung to Him (John 20:16–17). In Matthew 28:9 Jesus met the women as they returned from the tomb, and "they came and held Him by the feet and worshiped Him."

On several occasions, the resurrected Jesus ate food with His disciples. After walking with and teaching Cleopas and an unnamed disciple, we are told: "Now it came to pass, as He sat at the table with them, that He *took bread*, blessed and *broke it*, and *gave* it to them" (Luke 24:30, emphasis added). Peter later told the group gathered at the house of Cornelius: "Him God raised up on the third day, and showed Him openly, not to all the people, but to witnesses chosen before by God, even to us who ate and drank with Him after He arose from the dead" (Acts 10:40–41).

---

[8]   A close look at the temple cleansing accounts in the Gospels reveals that Jesus likely performed this action on two occasions: once at the start of His ministry and once in the week leading up to the Crucifixion. For more details on this subject, see my chapter in Ken Ham, Bodie Hodge, and Tim Chaffey, *Demolishing Supposed Bible Contradictions*, vol. 2 (Green Forest, AR: Master Books, 2012), pp. 129–135.

Perhaps the clearest passage on the subject describes Christ's appearance to His disciples, minus Thomas. Here, He convincingly proved that His resurrected body was the same body He had prior to the tomb.

> While they were saying these things, Jesus himself stood among them and said to them, "Peace be with you." But they were startled and terrified, thinking they saw a ghost. Then he said to them, "Why are you frightened, and why do doubts arise in your hearts? Look at *my hands* and *my feet*; *it's me*! *Touch me and see*; a ghost does not have *flesh and bones* like you see I have." When he had said this, he showed them *his hands* and *his feet*. And while they still could not believe it (because of their joy) and were amazed, he said to them, "Do you have anything here to eat?" So they gave him a piece of broiled fish, and *he took it* and *ate it* in front of them. (Luke 24:36–43, NET, emphasis added)

If Jesus merely rose in a "spiritual" body while His body that was placed in the tomb simply vanished, it is difficult to imagine the point of the Lord's actions in this passage. Why did He show them His hands and feet? Why did He tell them to touch Him and see? Why did He make it a point to show them that He was capable of eating food? Most confusing of all, why did He specifically tell them that He had "flesh and bones" if His resurrected body did not really have flesh and bones?

Eight days later, Jesus visited His disciples again, and this time Thomas was present. Jesus said to Thomas, "Reach your finger here, and look at My hands; and reach your hand here, and put it into My side. Do not be unbelieving, but believing" (John 20:27). Again, why would Jesus make a point of showing His wounds to the disciples and inviting Thomas to touch them if the body before them was not the same body that went into the tomb?

In the great Resurrection chapter, Paul addressed the following questions: "How are the dead raised up? And with what body do they come?" (1 Corinthians 15:35). Although he is specifically referring to the future resurrection of believers, Paul's response is completely relevant to Christ's resurrected body since our lowly bodies will become like His (Philippians 3:20; 1 John 3:2). To answer his own question, Paul uses an analogy of a seed, describing that "what you sow is not made alive unless it dies" (v. 36). He went on to explain how this is similar to our future resurrected bodies:

> So also is the resurrection of the dead. The body is sown in corruption, it is raised in incorruption. It is sown in dishonor, it is raised in glory. It is sown in weakness, it is raised in power. It is sown a natural body, it is raised a spiritual body. There is a natural body, and there is a spiritual body. And so it is written, "The first man Adam became a living being." The last Adam became a life-giving spirit. (1 Corinthians 15:42–45)

At first glance, this passage may seem to give some validity to the idea of a "spiritual" resurrection, since Paul mentioned a "spiritual body" (Greek: *pneumatikon sōma*). Doesn't this wording imply that the resurrected body is not physical? Actually, when applied to a human being in the New Testament, the word *sōma* (body) always refers to a physical body.[9]

Paul's point is that we will receive a spirit-dominated or spirit-controlled body, which is contrasted with our natural corrupt bodies.[10] Notice that it is the body that "is sown in corruption" that "is raised in incorruption" (v. 42). It is the body "sown in dishonor" that "is raised in glory" (v. 43). The body that "is sown in weakness" is the same one that "is raised in power." (v. 43). Finally, it is the "natural body" that "is raised [as] a spiritual body" (v. 44).

A few verses later Paul continues to expand on this idea.

> Now this I say, brethren, that flesh and blood cannot inherit the kingdom of God; nor does corruption

---

[9] Robert H. Gundry, *Sōma in Biblical Theology with Emphasis on Pauline Anthropology* (Cambridge: Cambridge University, 1976), p. 182.

[10] Norman L. Geisler, "In Defense of the Resurrection: A Reply to Criticisms, A Review Article" *Journal of the Evangelical Theological Society* 34, no. 2 (1991): 244.

inherit incorruption. Behold, I tell you a mystery:
We shall not all sleep, but we shall all be changed—in a
moment, in the twinkling of an eye, at the last trumpet.
For the trumpet will sound, and the dead will be
raised incorruptible, and we shall be changed. For this
corruptible must put on incorruption, and this mortal
must put on immortality. (1 Corinthians 15:50–53).

Once again, at first glance it may seem as if Paul lends support
to the spiritual resurrection position by claiming that "flesh and
blood cannot inherit the kingdom of God." However, the phrase
"flesh and blood" appears five times in the New Testament,
twice in the Septuagint, and is common in Rabbinic literature,
and it always carries "the primary sense of mortality rather than
physicality."[11] This is clear from the context too, since Paul wrote
that we shall all be changed—"this corruptible must *put on*
incorruption, and this mortal must *put on* immortality" (v. 53,
emphasis added). Our bodies will be changed, and the fact that
they must "put on" incorruption and immortality shows that the
believer does not receive an entirely new "spiritual body" while
the old rots in the ground.

Keeping Up Appearances

To support the position of a spiritual resurrection, adherents
often point to the confusion experienced by some of the witnesses
of the resurrected Savior. The two disciples on the Road to
Emmaus did not recognize Him until He broke bread with them
(Luke 24:30–31). Later that night, the disciples "were startled and
terrified, thinking they saw a ghost" (Luke 24:37, NET).

Supporters of the spiritual resurrection also claim that Jesus
was able to materialize within a locked room, thus demonstrating
that His "body" was not really physical. This idea is drawn primarily
from three passages. Luke 24:31 states that after the two disciples
recognized Him, "He vanished from their sight." A few verses later
we are told that the disciples were discussing the Resurrection, and
that "as they said these things, Jesus Himself stood in the midst of
them, and said to them, 'Peace to you'" (Luke 24:36). John wrote of

---

[11] Michael R. Licona, *The Resurrection of Jesus*, p. 418.

the same event, but added that "the doors were shut where the disciples were assembled, for fear of the Jews," and then "Jesus came and stood in [their] midst" (John 20:19).

The fact that Jesus vanished from the sight of two disciples does not prove that His body was immaterial. Consider that after Philip baptized the Ethiopian eunuch, "the Spirit of the Lord snatched Philip away; and the eunuch no longer saw him" (Acts 8:39, NASB). Furthermore, neither Luke nor John clearly state that Jesus simply materialized in the midst of the disciples or walked through a wall or locked door to appear to them. He may have done one of these things, but this still would not prove His immateriality.

Beckwith pointed out the key reason why these types of arguments for a spiritual resurrection fail to make a legitimate case for their position:

> The fundamental problem with Harris' defense is that he confuses ontology with epistemology—that is, he confuses Biblical statements about the being of Jesus' resurrected body with Biblical statements about the knowledge of the observers of Jesus' resurrected body. All the "materialistic" passages concern the being of his body (e.g. "Touch me and understand, because a ghost does not have flesh and bones, as you see I have" [Luke 24:39b]), while the "nonmaterialistic" passages concern the inability of the observers to see the risen Lord (e.g. "*He* disappeared from their sight" [Luke 24:31]). Some of the materialistic passages Harris cites (and one that is not cited [John 2:19–21]) have Jesus saying he is a body of flesh and bones. Yet it is interesting to note that Harris does not cite one nonmaterialistic passage in which Jesus says his body is immaterial; he merely cites passages in which Jesus cannot be seen. Granted that the nonmaterialistic passages tell us that Jesus' resurrected body is far different from an ordinary physical body (i.e. it is an immortal "spiritual" body), it is a logical *non sequitur* to say from this fact that it follows that Jesus' body is not physical.[12]

[12] Francis J. Beckwith, "Identity and Resurrection: A Review Article," *Journal of the Evangelical Theological Society* 33:3 (1990): 372.

Why Does It Matter?

To some readers, this debate may seem like theological hair-splitting. After all, both positions state that Jesus rose from the dead, so what's the big deal? There are several problems with the position advanced by Harris and Ladd, and the implications of adopting the "spiritual resurrection" position are quite profound.

First and foremost, this doctrine seriously calls into question the morality and integrity of the Son of God. As mentioned before, Jesus went to great lengths during His post-Resurrection appearances to demonstrate that He had risen from the dead. He ate and drank with His disciples, invited them to touch Him, and He specifically said that He had "flesh and bones" (Luke 24:39). Was Jesus deceiving His disciples by leading them to think He had a physical body? Certainly not!

Harris argued that "what [Jesus] wished them to understand (*idete*) by touching was not that he was material but that he was real."[13] This rationale reflects Harris' own ideas rather than those provided in the text.

Second, the notion of a spiritual resurrection makes no sense of the reaction of the Greeks to apostolic preaching on the Resurrection. When Paul spoke of the Resurrection in Athens, some Greek philosophers said that he seemed "to be a proclaimer of foreign gods" (Acts 17:18). Upon preaching in the Areopagus, Paul spoke of God raising Jesus from the dead as being "assurance" from God, implying a physical resurrection. When the Greeks "heard of the resurrection of the dead, some mocked" the idea (Acts 17:32). Paul apparently encountered the same sort of reaction within the Corinthian church, which explains why he spent a lengthy chapter dealing with the subject.[14] If Paul were merely describing a spiritual resurrection, the Greeks would have had little trouble with his preaching. In fact, that teaching would have been right in line with their thinking, since many of them

---

[13] Harris, *Raised Immortal*, p. 54.

[14] Licona cited D.B. Martin who surveyed "ancient beliefs regarding an afterlife and conclude[d] that the educated in that period did not believe in a resurrection of the body. Accordingly it was the educated believers in Corinth who refused to believe claims about the future resurrection of their bodies." Licona, *Resurrection of Jesus*, p. 419.

believed the spirit was pure and eternal while the body was evil
and needed to be discarded.

Third, Geisler rightly pointed out that God created the
physical body and pronounced it good. It was marred by sin,
which brought suffering and death. Paul explained that through
the death and Resurrection of Jesus, death and corruption will be
reversed (Romans 8:21–23). "But nothing less than a resurrection
in a physical body will restore God's original creation."[15]

Finally, this subject has a direct bearing on our eternal mode
of existence. Paul told the Philippians, "For our citizenship is
in heaven, from which we also eagerly wait for the Savior, the
Lord Jesus Christ, who will transform our lowly body that it may
be conformed to His glorious body. . . ." (Philippians 3:20–21).
John added that "when He is revealed, we shall be like Him, for
we shall see Him as He is" (1 John 3:2). These teachings concur
with Paul's words to the Corinthians that Christ's Resurrection
was a preview of our future resurrection.

> But now Christ is risen from the dead, and has
> become the firstfruits of those who have fallen asleep.
> For since by man came death, by Man also came the
> resurrection of the dead. For as in Adam all die, even
> so in Christ all shall be made alive. But each one in his
> own order: Christ the firstfruits, afterward those who are
> Christ's at His coming. (1 Corinthians 15:20–23)

Charles Wesley summarized the biblical teaching on the
likeness of our resurrected body to the Savior's quite well in his
classic hymn, "Christ the Lord Is Risen Today": "Made like Him,
like Him we rise, Alleluia!"

Conclusion

Jesus clearly demonstrated the material nature of His resurrected
body by eating and drinking with His disciples, inviting them to
touch Him, and even explicitly claiming that His body had flesh
and bones. These truths were taught by the apostles in Acts.
The epistles expand on these teachings, explaining that Christ's

[15] Geisler, "In Defense of the Resurrection," p. 245.

resurrected body provides us with a picture of what our future bodies will be like. To claim that Christ merely underwent a spiritual resurrection ignores clear biblical instruction and turns the post-Resurrection appearances of Christ into deceptive charades.

12 Did Someone Move the Body from the Tomb?

The first alternative view developed to explain away the Resurrection was that the disciples stole the body (Matthew 28:13). In fact, it was created on the same day that Jesus rose. This particular claim will be examined in detail in the next chapter. Realizing some of the weaknesses of the idea that the disciples were involved, skeptics have come up with similar ideas and some bizarre views to explain why the tomb was empty when the women visited it.

Dogs Ate the Body

Rather than specifically challenging the Resurrection accounts in Scripture, some have disputed the burial accounts of Jesus. This move essentially dodges the question of whether Jesus was raised in a glorified body. John Dominic Crossan, co-founder of the Jesus Seminar, has asserted that since Jesus was crucified His body would have either been left on the Cross to be torn apart by wild beasts or buried in a shallow grave and devoured by dogs. Regarding Christ's body Crossan wrote, "By Easter Sunday morning, those who cared did not know where it was, and those who knew did not care. Why should even the soldiers themselves remember the death and disposal of a nobody?"[1]

---

[1] John Dominic Crossan, *Jesus: A Revolutionary Biography* (New York, NY: HarperCollins, 1995), p. 158.

Crossan's proposal is fraught with problems. First, it is an argument from silence as he does not have a single ancient source to support his position. Citing what he believed normally happened to crucifixion victims does not guarantee that Jesus received the same treatment. What Crossan does cite are occasions when the bodies of crucifixion victims were left upon their crosses as a warning to all who might cross Rome. However, he does not acknowledge that these instances usually occurred in "times of acute crisis, when Roman military officers were being called in to stabilize situations which had gotten out of control."[2] Rome certainly had the prerogative to leave bodies on crosses, but they often allowed them to be buried.[3]

Second, contrary to Crossan's demeaning comment, Jesus was not a "nobody." His preaching and working of miracles had drawn the attention of thousands throughout Israel, including the Jewish authorities, who were quite interested in making sure His dead body was securely buried (Matthew 27:62–66).

Third, His death had a profound effect on the soldiers at the Cross who proclaimed, "Truly this was the Son of God" (Matthew 27:54; Mark 15:39). While Crossan would dismiss this statement, he cannot so lightly write off the evidence that Jesus was indeed buried in the tomb of Joseph of Arimathea (a rich man and member of the Jewish Council) since he accepts that the historical evidence shows that Jesus died by crucifixion. Many of these same documents assert that Jesus was buried in Joseph's tomb, and no contrary reports have been found. The earliest mention of Christ's burial is found in 1 Corinthians 15:4 and each of the four Gospels confirms that He was buried in Joseph's tomb. This argument perfectly illustrates Crossan's tendency to pick and choose which parts of Scripture he wants to believe and which he willfully rejects.[4]

---

[2] Byron R. McCane, "Where No One Had Yet Been Laid": The Shame of Jesus' Burial, in Bruce D. Chilton and Craig A. Evans, editors, *Authenticating the Activities of Jesus* (Boston, MA: Brill, 1998), p. 434. McCane's chapter effectively refutes Crossan's claim about the body remaining on the Cross.

[3] Ibid., pp. 435–436.

[4] For more information on Crossan's approach, see Tim Chaffey, "Should We Trust the Findings of the Jesus Seminar?" in Ken Ham and Bodie Hodge, gen. ed., *How Do We Know the Bible Is True?* vol. 2 (Green Forest, AR: Master Books, 2012), pp. 81–94.

Fourth, one of the historian's strongest criteria for accepting a testimony as legitimate is the existence of enemy attestation. That is, do one's enemies admit to the events in question? In this case, the Jewish authorities are said to have bribed Roman soldiers to report that Christ's disciples stole the body. It's true that Matthew is the only biblical writer to mention this idea, but it was still being taught for the next two centuries. In his *Dialogue with Trypho*, Justin Martyr (AD 100–165) spoke of this teaching being pushed in his day.

> . . . yet you not only have not repented, after you learned that He rose from the dead, but, as I said before, you have sent chosen and ordained men throughout all the world to proclaim that a godless and lawless heresy had sprung from one Jesus, a Galilæan deceiver, whom we crucified, but his disciples stole him by night from the tomb, where he was laid when unfastened from the cross, and now deceive men by asserting that he has risen from the dead and ascended to heaven.[5]

Several decades later, Tertullian (AD 160–225) acknowledged that this lie was still being used in his day. Paraphrasing his contemporaries who mocked Jesus, he wrote, "This is He whom His disciples secretly stole away, that it might be said He had risen again, or the gardener abstracted, that his lettuces might come to no harm from the crowds of visitants!"[6]

Crossan's position has no historical support, and he ignores any evidence contrary to his position. Yet there are strong historical reasons for believing Jesus was indeed buried in Joseph's tomb. Furthermore, Crossan's idea must depend upon other unreasonable scenarios to account for Christ's appearances to over 500 people. As such, the idea that dogs or other wild animals ate the Lord's body is without any merit.

---

[5] Justin Martyr, *Dialogue with Trypho*, chapter 108, cited in Philip Schaff, vol. 1, *The Ante-Nicene Fathers*, electronic ed. (Garland, TX: Galaxie Software, 2000).
[6] Tertullian, *De Spectaculis*, chapter 30, cited in Philip Schaff, vol. 3, *The Ante-Nicene Fathers*, electronic ed. (Garland, TX: Galaxie Software, 2000).

Reburial

An anti-Christian document called *Toledoth Jesu* proposed that Jesus was initially buried in Joseph's tomb. But when a gardener named Juda heard about the disciples' plans to steal the body of Jesus, he removed the body from the tomb and buried it in another grave. He informed the Jewish leaders and sold the body to them for 30 pieces of silver. Christ's body was then dragged through the streets of Jerusalem.[7]

This document might be somewhat disconcerting to many Christians had it been from the first century, but no scholar places its source material any earlier than the fourth century, and it probably was not penned until the tenth century. Jewish scholars have largely rejected this book as well because its contents are highly offensive, and they have traditionally taught a different view. And like the other views critiqued in this chapter, it does not provide any explanation for the appearances of the risen Lord to the disciples, James, and Paul.

Grave Robbers

Atheist Richard Carrier has promoted several alternatives to the Resurrection, including the idea that the body of Jesus was stolen from the tomb. He hastens to add that his essay "demonstrates the plausibility (but by no means the certainty) of the hypothesis that the body of Jesus was stolen."[8] Carrier does not really push for a specific culprit in such a theft. Essentially, he raises one argument from silence after another in an effort to claim that the hypothesis is feasible. He even goes so far as suggesting that the Resurrection account in Matthew is simply a "literary remodeling" of Daniel in the lion's den.[9]

Besides the fact that not one shred of historical evidence exists for Carrier's proposal, there are other difficulties to overcome. Did anyone have a motive to steal the body? As we'll see in the next chapter, the disciples cannot realistically be charged with this theft.

---

[7] Gary Habermas, *The Historical Jesus*, p. 205.
[8] Richard Carrier, "The Plausibility of Theft," in Robert M. Price and Jeffery Jay Lowder, editors, *The Empty Tomb: Jesus Beyond the Grave* (Amherst, NY: Prometheus Books, 2005), p. 349.
[9] Ibid., p. 362.

The Jewish and Roman leaders certainly would not have stolen the body without later unveiling it to stifle Christian preaching, nor did any of them ever make such a claim.

Carrier's idea is that occultists would have been interested in taking the skull of a holy man to perform their rituals. However, this practice is not known to have existed in Judea, and such thieves would not have taken the time to unwrap the body from the grave cloths and steal the entire body when all they allegedly wanted was a small part of it.[10] The church father, John Chrysostom (c. 347–407), demonstrated the absurdity of thieves unwrapping the body in the tomb.

> And what mean also the napkins that were stuck on with the myrrh; for Peter saw these lying. For if they had been disposed to steal, they would not have stolen the body naked, not because of dishonoring it only, but in order not to delay and lose time in stripping it, and not to give them that were so disposed opportunity to awake and seize them. Especially when it was myrrh, a drug that adheres so to the body, and cleaves to the clothes, whence it was not easy to take the clothes off the body, but they that did this needed much time, so that from this again, the tale of theft is improbable.[11]

Another difficulty with the theft idea is that the tomb was guarded by soldiers, so a thief would need to somehow perform his larceny without being noticed by people who were watching to make sure no one stole the body. Carrier appeals to Matthew 27:62 to point out that the guard was not set until the day after Jesus was buried, so "the whole night and part of the morning would still have been available for the unguarded body to be stolen."[12] It is true that the guard was not posted until the next day, but it is highly improbable that the soldiers who "went and

---

[10] J.P. Holding, *The Impossible Faith: Why Christianity Succeeded When It Should Have Failed* (Longwood, FL: Xulon Press, 2007), p. 104.

[11] John Chrysostom, Homilies on the Gospel According to St. Matthew, 90, cited in Philip Schaff, *The Nicene Fathers*, vol. 10, electronic ed. (Garland, TX: Galaxie Software, 2000).

[12] Carrier, "Plausibility," p. 358.

made the tomb secure [and sealed] the stone" (Matthew 27:66) would not have made sure the body was still in place—that is why they were specifically assigned to the tomb.

Carrier's hypothesis depends upon an incredibly inept group of soldiers. Matthew reports that after Jesus appeared to the women, the soldiers went back into Jerusalem and reported to the chief priests "all the things that had happened" (Matthew 28:11)—the tomb was now empty. But this raises some obvious questions. If the theft had occurred prior to the guards being stationed at the tomb, why was the massive stone now rolled away? The stone weighed an estimated three to four thousand pounds and was rolled down a slope by Joseph and Nicodemus to seal the tomb after they placed the body of Jesus inside (John 19:38–42).[13] Furthermore, were the soldiers so incompetent that they allowed someone to sneak past them and break in? Did the soldiers suddenly decide to break the emperor's seal and double-check to see if Christ's body was still in the tomb? No, when they secured the tomb they would have certainly made sure the body was present. And even if they had not, there is no legitimate way (other than the biblical reason) to explain why the tomb was opened during their watch.

Conclusion

Even if we were to grant this preposterous scenario any credibility, it would only explain why the tomb was empty. The stolen body hypothesis must rely upon other highly improbable or impossible views, such as the mass hallucination or vision theories, to explain the eyewitness testimony of the disciples that they had seen the risen Lord. Nor do the stolen body scenarios make sense of the conversions of James and Paul. They cannot provide an adequate explanation as to why the disciples were suddenly transformed into fearless proclaimers of the gospel.

Nevertheless, skeptics will continue to promote far-fetched hypotheses with no historical support in their efforts to justify their refusal to admit the truth of the Lord's Resurrection. They understand that if Jesus rose from the dead (and He did),

[13] Josh McDowell, A Ready Defense (Nashville, TN: Thomas Nelson, 1992), p. 226.

then He is the Son of God who will one day judge them for their rebellion. For the skeptic, this truth is unacceptable. Yet God is also merciful and gracious and will forgive and grant eternal life to all who turn to Him in faith.

13 Did the Disciples Steal the Body of Jesus?

As mentioned in the previous chapter, Justin Martyr and Tertullian reported that a common Jewish argument against the Resurrection was that the disciples stole the body of Jesus and then proclaimed He had risen from the dead. The Gospel of Matthew records this claim as well.

> Now while they were going, behold, some of the guard came into the city and reported to the chief priests all the things that had happened. When they had assembled with the elders and consulted together, they gave a large sum of money to the soldiers, saying, "Tell them, 'His disciples came at night and stole Him away while we slept.' And if this comes to the governor's ears, we will appease him and make you secure." So they took the money and did as they were instructed; and this saying is commonly reported among the Jews until this day." (Matthew 28:11–15)

Before highlighting the problems with this hypothesis, we need to identify the soldiers at the tomb. Were they part of the Jewish temple guard or were they Roman soldiers? The confusion on this point stems from Pilate's response to the request for the sealing of the tomb. He said to the chief priests and Pharisees, "You have a guard; go your way, make it as secure as you know how" (Matthew 27:65). At first glance, this would seem to indicate

Jewish guards; however, the words here are "grammatically ambiguous. They could be translated as a command, *have a guard*, making it probable that Pilate was giving the Jews temporary use of a group of Roman soldiers, or as a statement, *you have a guard*, making it more likely that he was telling the Jews to use their own temple police."[1] So which view is correct?

David MacLeod, in agreement with the majority of commentators, pointed out four reasons for taking the Greek word for "guard" in these verses (κουστωδία, *koustōdia*) as a reference to Roman soldiers.

> That it was Roman soldiers and not temple police who guarded the tomb is more likely for four reasons: First, they would not have needed Pilate's permission to use the temple police. Second, in [Matthew] 28:12 the soldiers are identified with the same word (στρατιώτης) used in [Matthew] 27:27, where the soldiers are undoubtedly Roman. Third, [Matthew] chapter 28 (v. 14) implies that the soldiers are answerable to Pilate. Fourth, the Greek can be understood to mean this.[2]

Let's look now at the multiple problems with the claim that the disciples stole the body. First, why would these men even attempt such a feat? They were on the run or in hiding (Mark 14:50) and did not expect Jesus to rise from the dead, "for as yet they did not know the Scripture, that He must rise again from the dead" (John 20:9; cf. Matthew 16:21–22; Luke 24:6–8; John 2:22). Although Jesus had told them on multiple occasions that He would die and rise again, the disciples did not understand His words because they, like their fellow Jews in those days, expected the Messiah to usher in an unending Jewish political kingdom. That the Messiah would die was far from their expectations. So when Jesus was crucified, the disciples were distraught and fearful.

---

[1] Craig Blomberg, *The New American Commentary: Matthew* (Nashville, TN: Broadman & Holman Publishers, 1992), p. 425. Emphasis in original.
[2] David J. MacLeod, "The Resurrection of Jesus Christ: Myth, Hoax, or History?" *Emmaus Journal*, Volume 7, Dubuque, IA: Emmaus Bible College (Winter 1998): 173.

Second, if the disciples were guilty of stealing the body of Jesus, why did they suddenly become fearless gospel preachers? If they knew their message was a sham, why would they be willing to endure continual persecution, imprisonments, and eventually martyrdom? As explained in chapter 4, liars don't make good martyrs. Some people may be willing to die for a lie, but *only if* they believe it to be true. However, to think that a group of men, with nothing to gain and likely everything to lose from an earthly perspective, would be willing to suffer and die for what they knew to be false strains credulity to the breaking point.

Third, how would a group of fishermen, a tax collector, and other members of the general public overpower or sneak past highly trained soldiers? A couple of possible answers come to mind. Like Carrier proposed, they stole the body before the guard was set the day after the Crucifixion. But this raises the exact same objections mentioned above and seriously calls into question the competency of a *koustōdia* of Roman soldiers.

Fourth, the other possible answer to the above question is precisely what the Jewish leaders bribed the soldiers to say: "His disciples came at night and stole Him away while we slept" (Matthew 28:13). Gromacki points out that the soldiers "had to be bribed because by telling a lie they would be putting their lives on the line. The Roman soldiers knew that to say that they were asleep when they should have been awake doing their duty would be to incriminate themselves. The penalty for a Roman soldier who slept while on guard was death. That is why the chief priests say that if the news reached the governor's ears, they would appease him and make the soldiers secure."[3]

With the guards asleep, the disciples just needed to be very quiet as they stole the body. The problem is that it is extremely unlikely that a group of Roman soldiers would fall asleep on the job given the fact that Roman soldiers would either be severely beaten or killed for falling asleep on the job. In his *Histories* the Greek historian Polybius (second century BC) described the rise of Rome and detailed the practices of the Roman legions.

[3] Gary R. Gromacki, "The Historicity of the Resurrection of Jesus Christ" *The Journal of Ministry and Theology*, Volume 6, Clarks Summit, PA: Baptist Bible Seminary (Spring 2002): 84.

He wrote that Roman soldiers who failed to perform their duties during night watches were subject to *fustuarium*, a punishment in which the guilty party attempted to run through a gauntlet of fellow soldiers striking him with cudgels and stones.

> Generally speaking men thus punished are killed on the spot; but if by any chance, after running the gauntlet, they manage to escape from the camp, they have no hope of ultimately surviving even so. They may not return to their own country, nor would any one venture to receive such an one into his house. Therefore those who have fallen into this misfortune are utterly and finally ruined.[4]

It is quite unthinkable that all of the guards would have fallen asleep on the job. They would have been well aware of the unrest in Jerusalem over Jesus, and they would have been certain to make sure no one broke that seal. But for the sake of argument, let's assume the Romans soldiers fell asleep guarding the tomb. Skeptics must assume that the disciples somehow quietly broke the Roman seal and silently rolled a massive stone away from the mouth of the tomb. Next, they must assume that the disciples took enough time in the tomb to unwrap the Lord's body and fold the face cloth (John 20:7). Then they must have carried the body out of the tomb without waking a single soldier.

Of course this entire scenario is absurd, but it gets worse (or better if you are a Christian). Keep in mind that this was the leading view of unbelievers in those days. It was the best explanation Christ's enemies could come up with. "His disciples came at night and stole Him away while we slept" (Matthew 28:13). Read it again. Did you catch the glaring contradiction in this theory? How would sleeping soldiers know who stole the body if their eyes were shut? The best skeptical view of the day refutes itself.

As Joseph informed his brothers, God often uses for good what men intend for evil (Genesis 50:20). Ironically, as David Turner noted, the posting and bribing of the Roman soldiers turned them into evangelists for the risen Savior.

---

[4] Polybius, *The Histories*, Perseus Digital Library, 6.36–37. Although Polybius lived more than a century prior to the time of Jesus, his writings provide insight into the strict discipline of the Roman legions.

In this passage the soldiers who were guarding Jesus' tomb became evangelists of Jesus' resurrection! Previously the leaders purported to need guards for fear that a resurrection hoax might occur, but those very guards later reported that a genuine resurrection had occurred. The leaders had outsmarted themselves: the very guards they secured to prevent a potential problem could not testify to an actual problem. So a "cover up" had to be concocted, and money must change hands to ensure that everyone had their story straight.[5]

Conclusion

The critics and skeptics who hold the moved or stolen body views propose that someone moved the body of Jesus before the tomb was found empty on that first Easter morning. As we will see in chapter 17, some skeptics have proposed even more outlandish tales, but such views go beyond special pleading and suffer from many of the same problems outlined in this chapter.

While each of these positions admits the first (Jesus was crucified) and the last (the tomb was empty) of the five minimal facts, none of them can account for the appearances of the risen Savior to more than 500 people, including the former skeptics James and Paul. As such, these highly improbable or impossible hypotheses must depend upon other implausible views, such as the hallucination or vision ideas. Thus, the moved body scenarios become weaker and weaker and eventually collapse under the weight of their own inadequacies and the eyewitness testimonies preserved in God's infallible Scripture.

Once again we see that the objections to the Resurrection are not based on the evidence. Instead, they are founded upon a determined effort to explain away what any open and honest investigator of the details would readily conclude: Jesus rose from the dead. Because the implications of this historical event completely destroy anti-Christian belief systems, the critics and skeptics have chosen to cling to baseless and often self-contradictory proposals

---

[5]   David Turner and Darrell L. Bock, *Cornerstone Biblical Commentary, Vol 11: Matthew and Mark* (Carol Stream, IL: Tyndale House Publishers, 2005), p. 374.

so they can continue in their rebellion against the Creator. While claiming to be rational, the skeptics have opted for irrational ideas to justify their unbelief. To believe in the resurrected Christ is a very reasonable faith. To deny the Resurrection after examining the evidence, one must either stick his head in the proverbial sand or take a blind leap into the dark.

14 Has the Family Tomb of Jesus Been Found?

Many critical New Testament scholars have pushed the idea that numerous versions of Christianity existed in the earliest years of the church. We are told by these liberal theologians that chauvinistic, power-hungry church leaders developed their own understanding of Christianity, squelching dissenting voices and destroying writings from these "competing Christianities" that did not conform to their narrow-minded dogmas. The books that survived this purge, they say, form what we call the New Testament today.

While these views of the early church and the formation of the canon are false, they have rapidly grown in popularity during the past century. The discovery of the Nag Hammadi Gnostic texts in 1945 helped prepare the fertile soil out of which these false views blossomed into the mainstream in the late twentieth century. The *Da Vinci Code*'s popularity (over 80 million copies sold worldwide) further promoted these lies.

This alternative "Christianity" that supposedly existed is not Christianity at all, but a counterfeit that would make envious the most radical revisionist historian. We are told that Jesus was really married to Mary Magdalene, never said anything offensive to sinners, did not die for the sins of the world, and did not rise bodily from the dead. It is this distorted form of "Christianity" that paved the way for the next alternate theory to the Resurrection that we need to examine.

The Jesus Family Tomb

On Sunday, March 4, 2007, the Discovery Channel aired *The Lost Tomb of Jesus*, a documentary produced by award-winning film director James Cameron featuring Simcha Jacobovici from the History Channel's *Naked Archaeologist* show and James Tabor, chair of the Department of Religious Studies at the University of North Carolina–Charlotte. They also released a book titled *The Jesus Family Tomb*. The program created quite a stir because these people claimed to have solid evidence that they had found the ossuary (bone box) of Jesus in a tomb in the Talpiot neighborhood of Jerusalem. One of the ossuaries in this tomb supposedly bore the inscription, "Jesus, son of Joseph."

Based on this discovery, the filmmakers wove a tale so profound that—were it true—would completely dismantle the Christian faith. Along with the Jesus ossuary, there were originally other bone boxes found, many of them bearing names closely connected with Jesus, such as Matthew, Mary, and Jose (shortened version of Joseph). Jacobovici claimed that the famous James ossuary (purported to be the bone box of the brother of Jesus) was the missing tenth ossuary from the Talpiot tomb. Perhaps even more volatile were claims that would be right at home in *The Da Vinci Code*. Allegedly, a bone box inscribed with the words "Mary the master" belonged to Mary Magdalene and a box marked "Judah, son of Jesus" belonged to the child of Jesus and Mary Magdalene.

Although many major media outlets push such radical ideas as representing true Christianity, the beliefs of modern critical scholars are far from biblical truth. A great illustration of how extreme their views are can be found in the comments of the co-founder of the Jesus Seminar. Although he has promoted other views to explain away the Resurrection, such as the claim that dogs ate the body (see chapter 12), John Dominic Crossan made the following comments in Jacobovici's film.

> If the bones of Jesus were to be found in an ossuary in Jerusalem tomorrow and without doubt let's say they are definitely agreed to be the bones of Jesus, would that destroy Christian faith? It certainly would not destroy

my Christian faith. I leave what happens to bodies up to God.[1]

Crossan's "Christian faith" is not Christian at all, since a denial of the bodily Resurrection of Jesus is actually a rejection of the Christian faith (1 Corinthians 15:12–21; Romans 10:9).

Thankfully, the Discovery Channel followed the documentary with *Lost Tomb of Jesus: A Critical Look*, a program hosted by Ted Koppel featuring Jacobovici and Tabor. There were also two teams of scholars consisting of archaeologists and theologians who discredited many of the claims made in the initial broadcast.

Koppel exposed the filmmakers for selectively editing comments from experts. In a Sourceflix production, *The Jesus Tomb Unmasked*, the following experts appearing in the original documentary expressed their frustration with being so heavily edited to make it sound as if they supported the claims of the documentary: Dr. Stephen Pfann (epigraphy), Steven Cox (forensic archaeologist), Dr. Shimon Gibson (archaeologist), and Dr. Amos Kloner (archaeologist). Each of these men rejects the hypothesis put forward by Jacobovici. Kloner led the original excavation of the Talpiot site in 1980 and stated emphatically that the tomb did not belong to Jesus Christ and blasted the film.

> Their movie is not serious. They [say they] are "discovering things." But they haven't discovered anything. They haven't found anything. Everything had already been published. And there is no basis on which to make a story out of this or to identify this as the family of Jesus.[2]

Besides the dubious, misleading, and sensationalist filmmaking practices, what are the problems with the actual hypothesis?

---

[1] Transcription of Crossan's comments in the film are from Charles Quarles, *Buried Hope or Risen Savior: The Search for the Jesus Tomb* (Nashville, TN: B&H Academic, 2008), pp. 10–11.
[2] Mati Milstein, "Jesus' Tomb Claim Slammed by Scholars." Available at <http://news.nationalgeographic.com/news/2007/02/070228-jesus-tomb.html>. Accessed January 25, 2013.

Dr. Kloner explains one of the major problems with this position.

> It makes a great story for a TV film. But it's completely impossible. It's nonsense. There is no likelihood that Jesus and his relatives had a family tomb. They were a Galilee family with no ties to Jerusalem. The Talpiot tomb belonged to a middle class family from the first century CE.[3]

Based on what we know about the family of Jesus from Scripture, Kloner's critique hits the mark. Even if Jesus did not rise from the dead, there are still multiple problems with identifying the Talpiot tomb with Jesus of Nazareth. One could propose that His family eventually moved to Jerusalem and either became wealthy or obtained a tomb from a wealthy person. But there are still problems.

The correlation of the names on the ossuaries is vastly overstated because each of the names was extremely common in Judea in the first century AD. Dr. Stephen Pfann, who appeared on the program and has studied the actual ossuary inscriptions, stated the following:

> They've evaluated this from the standpoint of the common person on the street rather than according to what the common person on the street, let's say, 2000 years ago would understand if you saw that there was a Jesus, son of Joseph. These are very, very common names, and it's kind of making the mountain out of a molehill type of thing.[4]

More specifically, consider just how popular these names were in Israel at the time:[5]

- Joseph/Joses was the second most popular male name.
- Judas/Yehuda was the fourth most popular male name.
- Jesus/Yeshua was the sixth most popular male name.

---

[3] David Horovitz interview with Amos Kloner cited in Quarles, *Buried Hope or Risen Savior: The Search for the Jesus Tomb*, p. 5.

[4] Interview with Dr. Stephen Pfann, Expedition Bible, *The Jesus Tomb Unmasked* DVD.

[5] Richard Bauckham, "The Names on the Ossuaries" in Quarles, *Buried Hope or Risen Savior*, p. 75.

- Matthew/Matthias was the ninth most popular male name.
- Mary was the most popular female name.
- Martha was the fourth most popular female name.

Conveniently, the filmmakers neglected to mention that two other ossuaries bearing the inscription "Jesus, son of Joseph" were found in the twentieth century.[6] They also misled viewers by giving a wildly speculative interpretation of the name "Mariamēnon" (one of the names on the ossuary) in claiming that this is Mary Magdalene. However, "there is no justification at all" for making this connection.[7]

Another problem for the filmmakers' hypothesis is that the so-called Jesus ossuary may not actually bear the name of Jesus at all. While the phrase "son of Joseph" is discernible, the etchings to the right are not so easy to read. Steve Caruso stated, "I cannot be even 10% conclusive about anything else in this inscription other than the name 'Joseph.'"[8] Dr. Pfann said that the name is probably Hanun instead of Jesus.[9]

Jacobovici made numerous reprehensible statements toward the Christian faith, but he also made a scandalous accusation against the original excavation team, implying that one of the members of this team stole the tenth ossuary from the tomb, which the filmmakers suggest was the James ossuary. This idea may be the most misleading of any of the forensic claims in the entire deceptive film. According to Dr. Gibson, the man in charge of sketching the ossuaries as part of the original expedition, the tenth ossuary found in the Talpiot tomb was broken, uninscribed, and undecorated, so it was not stored with the

---

[6]   Interview with Dr. Amos Kloner, Expedition Bible, *The Jesus Tomb Unmasked* DVD.

[7]   Bauckham, "The Names on the Ossuaries," p. 100.

[8]   Steve Caruso, "The Jesus Son of Joseph Inscription Part 2," The Aramaic Blog, March 29, 2007. Available at <aramaicdesigns.blogspot.com/2007/03jesus-son-of-joseph-inscription-part-2.html>. Accessed January 31, 2013. Caruso said he was 95% sure that the "Lost Tomb" proponents had correctly interpreted the *shin* (Hebrew letter giving the "sh" sound in Yeshua), but could not be more than 10% certain of anything else other than "Joseph."

[9]   Gary Habermas, *The Secret of the Talpiot Tomb: Unravelling the Mystery of the Jesus Family Tomb* (Nashville, TN: Holman Reference, 2007), p. 39.

inscription-bearing ossuaries. Yet the James ossuary is unbroken, inscribed, and decorated.[10] Furthermore, the two ossuaries have different dimensions. And if that were not enough, a photograph of the James ossuary was taken in 1976, but the Talpiot tomb was uncovered four years later.[11]

For Jacobovici to ignore the overwhelming evidence contrary to his view and suggest that the real archaeologists simply missed the inscription or failed to keep the box from being stolen is highly irresponsible and disgraceful. It would be hard not to conclude that he deliberately distorted the facts as a result of personal antipathy against Christianity.

One simple question should settle the matter of the so-called Jesus family tomb. If, as the filmmakers imply, the evidence overwhelmingly supports their claim to have found the remains of Jesus and His family, why did they resort to deception after deception to make their case? The fact is that this scenario preys on people who are ignorant of history, is based on sensationalism and fraud, and does not even approach making sense of the historical evidence. It does not even attempt to explain the empty tomb, "the infallible proofs" of the risen Jesus appearing to more than 500 people, or the conversions of Paul and James.

A Caution to Christians and Non-Christians Alike

Our society has provided a steady stream of supposed refutations of biblical truth. These often come from the Internet and popular media featuring friendly hosts, dazzling graphics, and authoritative-sounding pronouncements from experts. We need to be on our guard against these programs that seemingly prove the Bible wrong with their supposed "facts." The so-called Jesus family tomb was just another attempt in a long line of failed efforts to explain away the historical reality of the Resurrection of Jesus Christ. As we have seen, this hypothesis can easily be dismantled by a little bit of fact-checking.

---

[10] Interview with Dr. Shimon Gibson, Expedition Bible, *The Jesus Tomb Unmasked* DVD.
[11] Craig A. Evans, "The East Talpiot Tomb in Context" in Quarles, *Buried Hope or Risen Savior*, pp. 67–68.

Christianity is not a "blind faith" without historical grounding. Instead, it is a reasonable and defensible faith (Acts 17:2–3, 18:4; Jude 3). The next time you see or hear teaching that appears to contradict the Scriptures, remember that weak arguments, distortion of facts, and even outright deception are not uncommon practices for revisionist historians, atheists, and others seeking to prove Christianity wrong. The Bible has withstood these assaults throughout history, and it will survive the attacks of modern critical scholarship. No matter what rebellious people may say, we can be certain that Jesus Christ rose bodily from the grave and presented Himself alive by "many infallible proofs" (Acts 1:3).

Conclusion

In some ways, thinking about the so-called Jesus family tomb scenario reminds me of Psalm 2.

> Why do the nations rage, and the people plot a vain thing? The kings of the earth set themselves, and the rulers take counsel together, against the LORD and against His Anointed, saying, "Let us break Their bonds in pieces and cast away Their cords from us."
>
> He who sits in the heavens shall laugh; the LORD shall hold them in derision. Then He shall speak to them in His wrath, and distress them in His deep displeasure: "Yet I have set My King on My holy hill of Zion."
>
> "I will declare the decree: the Lord has said to Me, 'You are My Son, today I have begotten You. Ask of Me, and I will give You the nations for Your inheritance, and the ends of the earth for Your possession. You shall break them with a rod of iron; You shall dash them to pieces like a potter's vessel.'" (Psalm 2:1–9)

It is not only the angry and outspoken atheists who rage and plot vain things against God. Often the deadliest attacks come from mild-mannered and charming individuals like John Dominic Crossan and Simcha Jacobovici. Jesus warned about these types of false teachers, identifying them as wolves in sheep's clothing (Matthew 7:15). Paul warned the Ephesian elders of "savage wolves" who would speak "perverse things" to lead people astray (Acts 20:29–30). Yet no matter how prevalent man's deceptions become, God is always in control, His truth will always prevail, and one day He will crush all rebellion.

The solution for those who have been led astray is the same as it is for those wolves that have deceived them. Psalm 2 concludes with the following words:

> So now, you kings, do what is wise; you rulers of the earth, submit to correction! Serve the LORD in fear! Repent in terror! Give sincere homage! Otherwise he will be angry, and you will die because of your behavior, when his anger quickly ignites. How blessed are all who take shelter in him! (Psalm 2:10–12, NET)

The only way to avoid the coming wrath of God, which we all deserve for our rebellion against our Creator, is to repent of your sin and call out for forgiveness to the risen Savior Jesus Christ.

15 Did Jesus Really Die on the Cross?

One of the more popular alternate views among skeptics is called the swoon theory, which will be examined in more detail in the following chapter. Essentially, this view claims that Jesus somehow cheated death on the Cross, escaped the tomb, and then appeared to His disciples. This brings up an important question that must be answered first—can we really know if Jesus died on the Cross?

Roman Soldiers and Death

A major problem with the idea that Jesus did not die on the Cross is that it implies that Roman soldiers were too incompetent to determine whether or not Jesus was actually dead. However, the soldiers at the Cross would readily recognize the signs of death. After all, that was their job, they performed numerous crucifixions, which were designed to inflict tremendous agony leading up to death, and the Romans were lethally efficient.

Most Western people live in "sanitized" cultures where death is rarely witnessed. Even in the cases when we are in the presence of an individual when they die, the coroner soon arrives and takes the body. The next time we see the body, it has been carefully treated to make it presentable at a memorial service. So the notion that a person could fake death is perhaps somewhat believable in our culture. However, Roman soldiers would have been more than qualified to determine whether or not Jesus was dead. Yet proponents of the swoon theory must believe that the Roman centurion and other soldiers at the Cross were wrong in their pronouncement that Jesus was dead (Mark 15:44–45; John 19:33).

To speed death along, crucifixion victims would sometimes have their legs broken with an iron club in an act known as *crucifragium*.[1] On the day Jesus was crucified, the Jews requested this procedure so that the bodies would not remain on the crosses during the Sabbath (John 19:31). The soldiers broke the legs of the two thieves crucified along with Jesus, "but when they came to Jesus and saw that He was already dead, they did not break His legs" (John 19:33). Instead, one of the soldiers pierced His side with a spear. This important action will be discussed below.

Brutality of Crucifixion

By the time Jesus was nailed to the Cross, He would have been in an extremely poor condition and would have been unlikely to recover even if He had received a stay of execution. Let's briefly survey the physical torment Jesus endured in His final hours.

The Lord's suffering began with an intense "agony" while He prayed in the Garden of Gethsemane. His sweat fell "like great drops of blood" (Luke 22:44). This rare condition, known as *hematidrosis* or *hematohidrosis*, is caused by the rupture of tiny capillaries that feed the sweat glands, and is brought on by conditions of extreme physical or emotional stress.[2]

Next, Jesus was betrayed by Judas (Matthew 26:49), arrested and bound (John 18:12), and led to several illegal trials (Matthew 26:57).[3] In addition to being mocked, spat upon, and falsely accused during these overnight trials, Jesus was also brutalized as He was blindfolded, beaten, and struck in the face (Matthew 26:67–68; Mark 14:65; Luke 22:63–64).

---

[1] Gerald L. Borchert, *The New American Commentary: John 12–21* (Nashville, TN: Broadman & Holman Publishers, 2002), p. 273–274.

[2] Frederick Zugibe, *The Crucifixion of Jesus: A Forensic Inquiry*, 2nd ed. (New York, NY: M. Evans and Company, 2005), pp. 8–9.

[3] Robert Bucklin, M.D., J.D., explained that the Jewish leaders violated the following laws while handling the trials of Jesus: (a) no trials at night; (b) no trials during Passover, Sabbath, or the eve of either of these holy days; (c) defense attorney was not allowed; (d) the Sanhedrin could not bring the charges but only investigate them; (e) the Jews could not sentence someone to death since Rome reserved that right; and (f) they could not find two or three witnesses to agree. Robert Bucklin, "The Legal and Medical Aspects of the Trial and Death of Christ" *Medicine, Science, and the Law* 10 (January 1970): 14–26.

Despite the fact that Pilate declared Jesus to be innocent multiple times (John 18:38; 19:4, 6), He was still condemned to some of the harshest torture imaginable. Pilate ordered Jesus to be scourged. Piecing together elements from Luke and John, a number of scholars believe Jesus was whipped two separate times. The first occasion was the less severe form of flogging, known as *futigatio* (*paideusas* in Luke 23:16). Pilate hoped this beating would appease the Jews and he could then release Jesus since he could not find any fault in Him (Luke 23:14–15). John 19:1–15 reveals that this occurred prior to the crowd shouting for His Crucifixion and prior to the death sentence being handed down. Later, Pilate gave into the mob calling for crucifixion and had Jesus scourged, which was the severest form of flogging, known as *verberatio* (*phragellōsas* in Mark 15:15). Matthew 27:26 indicates that this occurred *after* Jesus was sentenced to be crucified.[4]

This ruthless form of whipping, *verberatio*, often killed its victims. Jesus would have been bound to a post while soldiers lashed Him using short whips (flagrums) made of several braided leather thongs with sharp pieces of metal, bones, or rocks tied into them. In their excellent treatment of the subject, Drs. Thompson and Harrub describe the gruesome results of flogging.

> The common method of Jewish scourging was via the use of three thongs of leather, the offender receiving thirteen stripes on the bare breast and thirteen across each shoulder (which explains the 40 stripes less one administered to Paul in 2 Corinthians 11:24). However, there was no such limit on the number of blows the Romans could deliver during a scourging, thus Christ's flogging at their hands would have been much worse. Christ would have received repeated blows to His chest, back, buttocks, and legs by two soldiers (known as lictors), the severity of which depended mainly on the mood of the lictors at the time. Initial anterior blows undoubtedly would

---

[4] A. N. Sherwin-White, *Roman Society and Roman Law in the New Testament* (Oxford University Press, 1963), pp. 27–28. See also Donald A. Carson, *The Pillar New Testament Commentary: The Gospel According of John* (Grand Rapids, MI: Eerdmans, 1991), pp. 596–597.

have opened the skin and underlying subcutaneous tissue of His chest (Davis, 1965, p. 185). Subsequent blows would have tattered the underlying pectoralis major and pectoralis minor muscles, as well as the medial aspects of the serratus anterior muscle (Netter, 1994, p. 174). Once these layers were ravaged, repetitive blows could fracture intercoastal [sic] ribs and shred the three layers of intercoastal [sic] muscles, causing superficial and cutaneous vessels of the chest to be lacerated. However we know that Christ did not suffer any broken bones because He was crucified in such a manner that "a bone of him shall not be broken" (John 19:36), as was foretold by earlier prophecies (cf. Exodus 12:46; Numbers 9:12; Psalm 34:20). Therefore, at best, the exposed superior epigastric artery and vein may have been compromised, while all other major anterior vessels would have been protected behind the ribs themselves (Netter, p. 175).[5]

Following the scourging, which often killed an individual, Jesus was further tormented. The Roman soldiers made a crown of thorns for His head. The thorns are traditionally thought to have come from the *Zizyphus spina christi* tree, but they could have also been from the date palm, both of which have thorns greater than an inch long.[6] This "crown" was not gently placed on Him. Instead the soldiers beat Him over the head with a staff, undoubtedly driving thorns into His scalp (Matthew 27:29–30, NET).[7]

Next, Jesus was led away to be crucified. Although popularly depicted as carrying both beams of the Cross, Jesus probably had to carry just the crossbeam, known as the *patibulum*, to "the Place of a Skull, which is called in Hebrew, Golgotha" (John 19:17). Battered and exhausted, Jesus could not carry it the entire distance, so the soldiers forced Simon of Cyrene to bear the beam for Him (Mark 15:21).

---

[5] Bert Thompson and Brad Harrub, "An Examination of the Medical Evidence for the Physical Death of Christ" available online at < http://www.apologetics-press.org/apcontent.aspx?category=13&article=145>. Accessed March 22, 2013.

[6] Carson, *The Gospel According of John*, p. 598.

[7] Many Bible translations render κάλαμον (*kalamon*) as "reed" instead of "staff" as in the NIV and NET. The Greek word can refer to either idea.

Upon arriving at Golgotha, Jesus refused the wine mixed with gall offered to Him, which would have helped deaden some of the pain. He was then nailed to the Cross. This would involve driving spikes through His wrists or hands and one long spike through both feet.[8] While on the Cross, Jesus would endure unimaginable torture as He struggled to breathe for the next six hours.[9]

Crucifixion was designed to be an extremely humiliating and painful form of execution. Victims were often stripped of their clothing and hung naked on the cross. In addition to fulfilling prophecy (Psalm 22:18), the fact that the soldiers cast lots for Christ's clothes (John 19:23–24) seems to imply that He was also crucified without any clothing.

Crucifixion was so agonizing that the word "excruciating" ("out of crucifying")[10] was coined to describe intense torment. Besides the severe injuries racking His body, Jesus also endured the shame of being wrongfully accused, as He was completely innocent of all charges. Likely worse than everything else, the perfectly holy Son of God suffered the unfathomable mental and spiritual anguish of bearing the wrath of God for the sins of the world (Isaiah 53:4–6; John 1:29; 2 Corinthians 5:21).

---

[8] There has been considerable debate about whether the spikes would be driven through His hands or His wrists, but that discussion is beyond the scope of this chapter. See Thompson and Harrub, "An Examination of the Medical Evidence for the Physical Death of Christ" for a helpful discussion on this point.

[9] Mark 15:25 indicates that Jesus was crucified at the "third hour" (9:00 AM) and Matthew 27:46–50 records that Jesus died about the "ninth hour" (3:00 PM). John may have made use of Roman timekeeping (John 19:14) rather than Jewish reckoning, although other possibilities have been presented to account for the differences in times provided in the Gospels. For a helpful survey of views on the timing discrepancy, see Carson, *Gospel According to John*, pp. 604–605 and Gerald L. Borchert, *The New American Commentary: John 12–21* (Nashville, TN: Broadman & Holman, 2002), pp. 257–258.

[10] *Excruciate* is from the "Latin *excruciatus*, past participle of *excruciare*, from *ex-* + *cruciare* to crucify, from *cruc-, crux* cross." Frederick C. Mish, Editor in Chief, *Merriam-Webster's Collegiate Dictionary*, Eleventh Edition (Springfield, MA: Merriam-Webster, 2008), s.v. "excruciate."

The Spear in the Side

After Jesus breathed His last, a soldier "pierced His side with a spear, and immediately blood and water came out" (John 19:34). This unexpected detail in John's account destroys any possibility of Jesus faking His own death. Medical examiner Dr. Alexander Metherell explained why "blood and water came out":

> Even before He died...the hypovolemic shock would have caused a sustained rapid heart rate that would have contributed to heart failure, resulting in the collection of fluid in the membrane around the heart, called a pericardial effusion, as well as around the lungs, which is called a pleural effusion. The spear apparently went through the right lung and into the heart, so when the spear was pulled out, some fluid—the pericardial effusion and the pleural effusion—came out. This would have the appearance of a clear fluid, like water, followed by a large volume of blood, as the eyewitness John described in his gospel. John probably had no idea why he saw both blood and a clear fluid come out—certainly that's not what an untrained person like him would have anticipated. Yet John's description is consistent with what modern medicine would expect to have happened.[11]

John apparently recognized the strangeness of his report. Throughout his recounting of Christ's arrest, trials, and execution, John delivered detail after detail, explaining what Jesus had gone through. Then immediately after mentioning the "blood and water," John stopped his narration of events to stress to his readers that he really saw blood and water flow from Christ's side. He wrote, "And he who has seen has testified, and his testimony is true; and he knows that he is telling the truth, so that you may believe" (John 19:35). It's almost as though John was telling his readers, "I know this is really strange, but I'm not lying, I really saw blood and water flow." And perhaps unbeknownst to John, this brief verse provides modern medical doctors with evidence

---

[11] Dr. Alexander Metherell in an interview with Lee Strobel, *The Case for Christ* (Grand Rapids, MI: Zondervan, 1998), p. 199.

that demolishes the swoon theory and any other position that claims Jesus did not die on the Cross.

Conclusion

In addition to attacking the character of the Son of God, those who claim that Jesus somehow survived Crucifixion ignore numerous key factors. They deny the first minimal fact accepted by the vast majority of historians—Jesus died by Crucifixion. They reject the clear words of eyewitness testimony recorded in Scripture. They seem to be ignorant of the extreme brutality of crucifixion. They slander the competence of the Roman soldiers at the Cross who were charged with executing Jesus. Finally, they are at odds with many detailed studies of medical experts whose research has led them to agree with the Gospel writers that Jesus died by Crucifixion.

16 Did Jesus Fake His Own Death?

The Bible states that Jesus died by Crucifixion. This is corroborated by historians of all stripes and medical experts. In their efforts to account for the post-Resurrection appearances, some critics have developed elaborate schemes in which Jesus somehow managed to escape the Cross with His life.

The Swoon Theory

Proposed by Heinrich E.G. Paulus in *The Life of Jesus* (1828), the swoon theory states that Jesus was not actually dead when He was removed from the Cross. Instead, He had fallen into a coma-like state (a swoon) on the Cross and was then buried in a tomb in that condition. He later revived, rolled away the stone from the inside, evaded the Roman guards, and escaped. He then appeared to His disciples proclaiming He had conquered death. But rather than making a full recovery, Jesus died soon thereafter due to His numerous injuries.

In his popular book, *The Passover Plot* (1969), radical New Testament scholar Hugh J. Schonfield attempted to resurrect the swoon theory with some modifications. He proposed that Jesus set out to fulfill the Old Testament's messianic prophecies. According to Schonfield's version of the swoon theory, Jesus enlisted the aid of men like Joseph of Arimathea and Lazarus of Bethany to help Him accomplish an elaborate hoax. Joseph arranged for an unidentified person to give Jesus a drink on the Cross that would cause Him to lose consciousness and appear to be dead. However, no one involved in the scheme anticipated the spear wound, which gravely injured Jesus. He was removed from the tomb the next day and briefly regained consciousness before dying and being reburied elsewhere.

Schonfield admitted the imaginative nature of his work when he wrote, "We are nowhere claiming for our reconstruction that it represents what actually happened, but that on the evidence we have it may be fairly close to the truth."[1] He also had the audacity to claim that the image of Jesus which emerges from his book "does not, when honestly examined, detract from his greatness and uniqueness."[2] Frankly, it is beyond absurd to think that demoting the sinless Son of God to a deceitful, scheming, wannabe Messiah does not detract from Christ's greatness and uniqueness.

Did Jesus Fake His Death?

Neither the swoon theory nor its stepchild, the Passover plot, can account for the evidence, although these views cleverly attempt to bypass Christ's death by crucifixion, claiming that He merely deceived others into thinking He had died. So these views rely upon Jesus being a very clever deceiver and a fraud. This is certainly a different view of Jesus than most scholars hold—even many ardent skeptics admit that Jesus was highly moral.

These two views cannot account for three of the five minimal facts: the appearances to the disciples and the conversions of James and Paul based on their beliefs they had seen the risen Lord. Both the swoon theory and the "Passover Plot" require that Jesus not only somehow survived the Crucifixion, but He also must have recovered from the brutal torture leading up to the Crucifixion and from the Crucifixion itself, at least for a long enough time to make a few appearances.

Ingenious conspiracy theories often convince those who are ignorant of history, particularly of the details of flogging and crucifixion. But there are good reasons why no one in the ancient world proposed that Jesus survived the Crucifixion and why even the "historical Jesus" scholars acknowledge that Jesus died on the Cross. Simply put, the Romans were experts at executing people, and to

[1] Hugh J. Schonfield, *The Passover Plot* (New York: Bantam Books, 1969), p. 165.
[2] Ibid., p. 7.

think that someone could survive the horrors Jesus endured displays either the critics' willful ignorance or their desperate attempt to deny the obvious.

The Mighty Death Conqueror or the Mighty Fraud?

The swoon theory enjoyed popular support among liberals for several decades after being introduced in 1828. That all changed when another liberal theologian, David F. Strauss, delivered a fatal blow to the view in *A New Life of Jesus* (1865).

> It is impossible that a being who had stolen half-dead out of the sepulchre, who crept about weak and ill, wanting medical treatment, who required bandaging, strengthening and indulgence, and who still at last yielded to his sufferings, could have given to his disciples the impression that he was a Conqueror over death and the grave, the Prince of Life, an impression which lay at the bottom of their future ministry. Such a resuscitation could only have weakened the impression which he had made upon them in life and in death, at the most could only have given it an elegiac voice, but could by no possibility have changed their sorrow into enthusiasm, [and] have elevated their reverence into worship.[3]

Let's pretend that against all odds, the biblical affirmation, common sense, and medical expertise, Jesus somehow managed to survive the Crucifixion. After being taken down from the Cross, His body was wrapped in linen cloths, along with a "mixture of myrrh and aloes, [weighing] about a hundred pounds" (John 19:39). It was then sealed in a cold, dark tomb behind a massive stone. Consider what would still need to occur if Jesus was somehow still alive at this point. He would have to revive in the tomb, unwrap Himself from the linen cloths, roll away the huge stone (weighing an estimated 1–2 tons) from the inside of the tomb (a job that required multiple people from outside the tomb), sneak past the guards (or beat them all up), and then appear to the disciples to convince them that He had conquered death.

---

[3] David Friedrich Strauss, *A New Life of Jesus* (in Two Volumes), Vol. 1 (London: Williams and Norgate, 1865), p. 412.

But remember, Jesus would not have been able to walk because of the injuries caused by the spike through His feet. Nor would He have been able to crawl on His hands, let alone use them to roll away the stone, since His hands or wrists had just been pierced with spikes. At best, He could perform some sort of military crawl, but even this type of movement would have been acutely painful considering His other injuries caused by the spear and the scourging.

As Strauss pointed out, no sane person would mistake a barely-clinging-to-life Jesus as the mighty, death-conquering Son of God and then risk life and limb to promote Him as the long awaited resurrected Messiah. If anything, seeing their master in such a pitiful state as a result of his elaborate plan gone wrong, the disciples would reject Him outright as a fraud. Yet according to church history, every one of Christ's apostles faced death or exile for their message. So neither the swoon theory nor the Passover plot can account for the dramatic change in the lives of the disciples. The faked death views also fail to account for the conversions of the former skeptics, James the half-brother of Jesus and Saul of Tarsus.

Conclusion

Much more could be written concerning the suffering Jesus endured in His final hours. The proposal that Jesus survived the Cross betrays an ignorance of the brutality of Crucifixion, depends upon unbelievably incompetent soldiers at the Cross, fails to account for the evidence, and cannot explain why the disciples would willingly die for their belief that Jesus had risen from the dead.

Identifying Jesus as a fraud is nothing new; some of His contemporaries claimed He was a deceiver. John 7:12 states, "And there was much complaining among the people concerning Him. Some said, 'He is good'; others said, 'No, on the contrary, He deceives the people.'" Now 2,000 years later, rebellious men still charge Jesus with deception.

Isn't it interesting that the subject of Jesus causes so much stress and discomfort to those who claim He was just a fake? Why would they worry so much about Him? Yet the power of Christ's Crucifixion and Resurrection still converts sinners to saints, sobers drunks, gives hope to many millions, and saves men and women from lives of sin and eternal destruction. Understanding the extent of torture Jesus endured for us helps us appreciate even more "the width and length and depth and height" (Ephesians 3:18) of the love God has shown to us by sending His Son to die in our place. The Father "made Him who knew no sin to be sin for us, that we might become the righteousness of God in Him" (2 Corinthians 5:21). We do not deserve the grace, mercy, and love God has shown us. Instead, we deserve to bear the punishment Jesus endured and should be separated from God forever because of our sinfulness.

Sadly, many people scorn the gracious offer of eternal life and often resort to unreasonable ideas like the swoon theory to justify their unbelief. If you are an unbeliever, I urge you to turn from your rebellious ways and call on the mighty Death Conqueror, Jesus Christ. He is the only one who can save you from your sins and is the only hope for this world.

17 Can Some of the Less Popular Views Explain Away the Resurrection?

Over the past several chapters we have critiqued the leading alternative hypotheses that have been developed in attempts to explain away the Resurrection of Jesus. Each of these ideas contradicts Scripture, and each is woefully inadequate at explaining all of the facts. Instead, we have seen that historical and archaeological evidences are perfectly consistent with Christ's conquering of death recorded in God's Word. Nevertheless, many critics and skeptics have remained undaunted and sometimes resort to even more outlandish theories to justify their unbelief. This chapter will examine four lesser-known attempts to deny the Resurrection. For reasons that will become obvious, these views have gained very little traction among skeptical and critical scholars, but they highlight just how desperate some unbelievers are to keep Jesus in the tomb.

Wrong Tomb

Kirsopp Lake (1872–1946), a critical New Testament professor, suggested that the women simply went to the wrong tomb, assumed that He rose from the dead, and then ran away. They eventually told the disciples about their encounter with an empty tomb, which led to the disciples experiencing visions of the risen Lord. He wrote the following:

> The women came in the early morning to a tomb
> which they thought was the one in which they had seen

the Lord buried. They expected to find a closed tomb, but they found an open one; and a young man, who was in the entrance, guessing their errand, tried to tell them that they had made a mistake in the place. "He is not here," said he, "see the place where they laid him," and probably pointed to the next tomb. But the women were frightened at the detection of their errand, and fled, only imperfectly or not at all understanding what they heard."[1]

Lake's proposal has not gained a following since it is beset with so many obvious problems.

First, Lake conveniently omitted some words from his quotation of Mark 16:6, but had he cited the rest of the verse, his hypothesis would have immediately crumbled. Mark actually wrote, "But he said to them, 'Do not be alarmed. You seek Jesus of Nazareth, who was crucified. *He is risen!* He is not here. See the place where they laid Him'" (Mark 16:6, emphasis added).

Second, this view does not provide any explanation for the disciples' belief that they had actually seen, eaten food with, and touched the risen Lord. These "infallible proofs" (Acts 1:3) cannot be ignored if someone intends to propose a viable alternative to the biblical explanation of Christ's Resurrection. Furthermore, the empty tomb was not what convinced Christ's followers that He had risen from the dead;[2] it was the physical appearances of the Savior that won them over.

---

[1] Kirsopp Lake, *The Historical Evidence for the Resurrection of Jesus Christ* (New York: G.P. Putnam's Sons, 1907), pp. 251–252.

[2] A possible exception to this is John. Some scholars conclude that he believed in the Resurrection upon seeing the grave clothes in the otherwise empty tomb. This is based on John 20:8, which states, "Then the other disciple, who came to the tomb first, went in also; and he saw and believed." See, for example, John F. MacArthur, *The MacArthur Study Bible* (Nashville, TN: Thomas Nelson, 1997), note on John 20:8. Others think that at this point "the other disciple" (almost certainly John himself) had believed Mary Magdalene's claim that someone had moved the body out of the tomb to an unknown location (John 20:2). Support for this interpretation is found in John's next verse, "For as yet they did not know the Scripture, that He must rise again from the dead" (John 20:9). Also, John does not distinguish himself from the other disciples in John 20:20 who did not believe Jesus was risen until they saw the evidence of His hands and side. Even if John did believe at this point, the empty tomb was not what convinced the remaining disciples of the Resurrection.

Third, even if the women went to the wrong tomb, the proclamation of the empty tomb would not persuade skeptics like James and Paul. Paul would have simply assumed that somebody moved the body, since that was the explanation of the Jewish leaders at the time. It was the post-Resurrection appearances that convinced these former skeptics.

Fourth, Lake's proposal does not explain what fresh grave cloths were doing in the wrong tomb. Did somebody else just rise from the dead out of that wrong tomb? Was someone else's body recently stolen from that tomb?

Fifth, it is conceivable that the women could have gone to the wrong tomb in the wee hours of the morning. But the Bible tells us that "Mary Magdalene and Mary the mother of Joses observed where He was laid" (Mark 15:47), and it is highly unlikely that they would both forget in three days where the one they loved was buried. Furthermore, even in the unlikely event that the women went to the wrong tomb, we must wonder why two angels visited the wrong tomb, why Peter and John ran to the wrong tomb, and why Roman soldiers guarded the wrong tomb (Matthew 28:1–4). Believing that this alleged mistake could spark the Christian movement is unreasonable. The early Christians claimed that Jesus was buried in a tomb, and not just any tomb, but the tomb of Joseph of Arimathea, a member of Israel's Great Sanhedrin and secretly a disciple of Jesus (John 19:38). Surely, he could have remembered where his own tomb was.

Furthermore, as the Christian faith began to spread throughout Jerusalem, the Jewish leaders could have easily ascertained from Joseph where his tomb was (if they didn't already know). And if the Resurrection were just a hoax, they could have produced the body of Jesus and paraded it on a cart through the streets of Jerusalem. Christianity would have ended as soon as it began. Instead, as discussed in chapter 13, the Jewish leaders of the day agreed to promote with the Roman soldiers an explanation that they knew was false—that the disciples had stolen the body (Matthew 28:11–15).

Annihilation

In 1959, G. D. Yarnold described a fanciful hypothesis in his book *Risen Indeed*. According to Yarnold, "the material body of the Lord ceased to exist, or was annihilated."[3] This view has gained very little support for obvious reasons.

First, there is no support for such a claim, and it comes across as terribly *ad hoc*. No one has proposed any logical reasons why the body of Jesus would simply cease to exist in the tomb. Even if the highly questionable idea known as spontaneous human combustion (SHC) is proposed to explain the annihilation of the body, it would not apply here. In those odd cases identified by some as SHC, the charred remains of the individual are found, so this would not match the annihilation proposal.

Second, the annihilation proposal acknowledges that the tomb was empty, yet gives what amounts to an argument from silence to explain how it was vacated. As far as we know, the total annihilation of a body leaving no remains would be entirely unique. To annihilate the body and yet leave the grave clothes would be even more astoundingly unique. Only God could do such a thing—natural processes surely aren't up to the task. But the only true God, the God of the Bible, clearly says in His Word that He raised Jesus from the dead. He did not annihilate Christ's body.

Those who believe in the Resurrection of Jesus can point to Christ's prophetic statements that He would rise (Matthew 12:39–40, 16:21, 20:18–19; John 2:19–22), and Scripture describes at least eight other individuals who were raised from the dead, so there is precedent for such an event, particularly associated with Jesus.[4]

---

[3] G. D. Yarnold, *Risen Indeed: Studies in the Lord's Resurrection* (New York: Oxford, 1959), p. 22. Cited in Merrill C. Tenney, *The Reality of the Resurrection* (Chicago, IL: Moody Press, 1972), n.p. Electronic version of the chapter in which this statement appears is available from <www.rediscoveringthebible. com/Realitych6.pdf>. Accessed February 1, 2013.

[4] For the accounts of people raised from the dead see 1 Kings 17:17–24; 2 Kings 4:8–37, 13:20–21; Luke 7:11–15, 8:49–56; John 11; Acts 9:37–40, 20:9–12. Each of these people was raised in their own earthly body and would eventually die again, while Jesus was raised in a glorified body and can never die again. Some believe that Jonah died while in the great fish (Jonah 2:2–6; cf. Matthew 12:39–40). Also, Matthew 27:52–53 is an intriguing passage describing the raising of many saints at the time of Christ's death. See chapter 21 for more details.

It is special pleading to suggest that the one person in all of human history whose body was annihilated after death just happened to be Jesus—the single most influential person who has ever lived, whose exclusive claims have incurred the animosity of millions, and who "just happened" to predict His own death, burial, and Resurrection.

Finally, the annihilation view cannot account for three of the five minimal facts—the reported appearances to the disciples, the conversion of James, and the conversion of Saul of Tarsus. At best, this position only gives a highly unreasonable justification for the empty tomb, but it must rely on one or more of the other flawed views to explain the appearances.

Séance

The séance view suggests that "the personality of the dead Christ was reproduced through a medium or else manifested itself by ectoplasm [the vaporous, luminous substance believed by spiritualists to emanate from a medium in a trance]."[5] Like the annihilation view, hardly anyone accepts this proposal because, in addition to questionable paranormal activity, there are just too many problems.

First, the anti-supernatural skeptics cannot adopt this view since it relies upon a metaphysical explanation for the Resurrection. If they were to grant legitimacy to this view it opens the door for other supernatural explanations, such as the biblical view.

Second, it assumes that the disciples, devout Jews who were not even looking for the resurrected Savior, engaged in a practice strictly forbidden in the Old Testament.

> When you come into the land which the LORD your God is giving you, you shall not learn to follow the abominations of those nations. There shall not be found among you anyone who makes his son or his daughter pass through the fire, or one who practices witchcraft, or a soothsayer, or one who interprets omens, or a sorcerer, or one who conjures spells, or a medium, or a spiritist, or one who calls up the dead. For all who do these things

---

5 Tenney, *Reality*, p. 189.

are an abomination to the LORD, and because of these abominations the LORD your God drives them out from before you. (Deuteronomy 18:9–12)

Third, the séance view does not account for the empty tomb, since the body of Jesus would have remained in place. Nor does it provide an adequate explanation for the appearances to skeptics like James or Paul. Surely Paul, a law-abiding Pharisee (Philippians 3:5–6) who persecuted Christians to death (Acts 22:4), would not seek to contact the spirit of Jesus via a séance.

Finally, the descriptions of the Resurrection appearances do not even come close to matching some sort of ectoplasmic phantasm allegedly called up during a séance. While the Bible possibly provides an example of this type of occult activity (1 Samuel 28:3–25), the circumstances and descriptions of King Saul consulting a medium are very different than the appearances of the resurrected Jesus. According to Scripture, Jesus appeared to people in a variety of locations, including near the tomb, a roadway, a hillside, the seashore, a locked house, and the Mount of Olives.

Aliens Stole the Body
Seriously?

Conclusion
We have completed our examination of the alternative hypotheses developed by critics and skeptics in their efforts to deny the Resurrection of Jesus Christ. These views all contradict the inerrant Word of God and fall woefully short of explaining the evidence. In fact, every argument raised against the knowledge of God (2 Corinthians 10:5) will crumble just like these alternative theories have. Falsehoods cannot stand, but the Word of God will stand forever (Isaiah 40:8; Matthew 24:35).

Christians can take comfort in knowing that Jesus not only died for their sins, but He also rose from the dead a few days later. These core Christian truths have been attacked for centuries by leading critics and skeptics. But even their best explanations pose no threat to the truth and reveal that they are merely grasping at straws in a futile attempt to excuse their sin and justify their unbelief.

On the other hand, unbelievers should be quite concerned. If Jesus rose from the dead (and He did), then He is precisely who He claimed to be—the Son of God who will one day return in judgment against sinners (Matthew 26:63–64; 2 Timothy 4:1). If you are an unbeliever, take a close look at the best alternatives your fellow unbelievers have developed in response to the Resurrection.

- Mistaken Identity
- Legend
- Copycat
- Hallucinations
- Visions
- Dogs Ate the Body
- Reburial
- Grave Robbers
- Disciples Stole the Body
- The Jesus Family Tomb
- Swoon Theory
- Passover Plot
- Wrong Tomb
- Annihilation
- Séance

Here's my question for you. Which one? Which one of these flawed and unsubstantiated views are you placing your faith in? Which one are you clinging to in hopes that you won't have to face the risen Lord and Savior Jesus Christ on Judgment Day? The Bible provides a glimpse of what your future meeting with Jesus will entail.

> Therefore God also has highly exalted Him and given Him the name which is above every name, that at the name of Jesus every knee should bow, of those in heaven, and of those on earth, and of those under the earth, and that every tongue should confess that Jesus Christ is Lord, to the glory of God the Father. (Philippians 2:9–11)

One way or another, every person will bow the knee before Jesus and confess that He is Lord. Please don't wait until it is too late. You do not know when you will draw your last breath or when Jesus will return. If you neglect His salvation until then, you will still bow before Him and confess Him as Lord, but you will then face His wrath, suffering eternally for your sins against the infinitely holy God. I urge you to do it now willingly—turn from your sins and call upon the risen Jesus to save you from His coming judgment, and then enter into the joy of personally knowing the good, loving, merciful, gracious, kind, faithful, all-powerful, all-knowing, holy, majestic, eternal, sovereign Creator of heaven and earth.

> That if you confess with your mouth the Lord Jesus and believe in your heart that God has raised Him from the dead, you will be saved. (Romans 10:9)

Section Three:
Other Relevant Questions

18 Are There Contradictions in the Resurrection Accounts?

Skeptics often seize upon differences in the biblical accounts and cry "Contradiction!" For example, one author cited 13 alleged contradictions in the Resurrection accounts, but nearly all of these consist of a detail recorded in one Gospel but not in the others. We are told that since the Gospel writers could not keep their stories straight, we should throw out their claims about the Resurrection. Of course, this does not constitute a contradiction.

From a logical perspective, even if there were contradictions in these accounts, it would not falsify the Resurrection, since Christ's rising from the dead does not depend on the complete accuracy of the Gospel accounts—it depends on whether He actually rose. If there were contradictions in the original manuscripts, it would be a strike against inerrancy, but it does not follow that it would prove Jesus did not rise. Nevertheless, I do not believe there are any contradictions in these accounts. If I'm correct, then the critics' argument is moot. Let's take a look at some of these alleged contradictions. The charges covered in this chapter will be pretty basic, while the next chapter will explain how the appearances of the risen Savior are not contradictory at all.

How Many Women Went to the Tomb and at What Time?

One of the easiest of the alleged contradictions to answer is the claim that the biblical writers could not even figure out how many women went to the tomb or at what time they arrived. Here is what we are told in each of the Gospels:

> Now after the Sabbath, as the first day of the week began to dawn, Mary Magdalene and the other Mary came to see the tomb. (Matthew 28:1)

> Now when the Sabbath was past, Mary Magdalene, Mary the mother of James, and Salome bought spices, that they might come and anoint Him. Very early in the morning, on the first day of the week, they came to the tomb when the sun had risen. (Mark 16:1–2)

> Now on the first day of the week, very early in the morning, they, and certain other women with them, came to the tomb bringing the spices which they had prepared…It was Mary Magdalene, Joanna, Mary the mother of James, and the other women with them, who told these things to the apostles. (Luke 24:1, 10)

> Now the first day of the week Mary Magdalene went to the tomb early, while it was still dark, and saw that the stone had been taken away from the tomb. Then she ran and came to Simon Peter, and to the other disciple, whom Jesus loved, and said to them, "They have taken away the Lord out of the tomb, and we do not know where they have laid Him." (John 20:1–2)

The so-called contradictions here are really just apparent disagreements. That is, from a cursory glance there appears to be some contradictions, but as we look a little closer, we see that these passages fit together nicely.

Each of the Gospels state that Mary Magdalene went to the tomb, and they agree that she was not alone. John does not name another person with her, but quotes her as saying, "...we do not know where they have laid Him." Matthew mentions another Mary—this may have been Mary the wife of Clopas who was at the Cross (John 19:25) or it may have been Mary the mother of James, named by both Mark and Luke. Mark places Salome there and Luke adds that Joanna was among them too. Since Luke names three women (Mary Magdalene, Joanna, and Mary the mother James) and adds that there were "other women with them," we know there were at least five women who went to the tomb.

This is a case where none of the Gospels provide all of the details, but the passages each provide partial information that gives us a fuller picture of what happened. Notice that none of the writers claim that there was *only* one woman or *only* two women that went to the tomb, so there is no contradiction here.

Is there a contradiction in the timing of this event? Not at all. Matthew says that the women came to the tomb as the first day of the week "began to dawn." Mark stated, "Very early in the morning, on the first day of the week, they came to the tomb when the sun had risen." Luke adds that they came to the tomb "very early in the morning." While it is very easy to reconcile the very slight differences in wording in these three accounts, it is the Gospel of John that seems to throw a wrench into the works. John wrote, "Mary Magdalene went to the tomb early, while it was still dark."

There are at least two plausible solutions to this dilemma. All of the accounts agree that it was quite early on the first day of the week when the women arrived at the tomb (Sunday). One solution is that the terms used by the writers each describe what it is like at daybreak. It is "still dark" in much of the sky "very early in the morning" when the sun begins creeping above the horizon. A second solution is that John described the moment the women set out as being "still dark" while the other writers describe the position of the sun in the sky when the women arrived at the tomb. Either of these solutions are reasonable, and there may be other viable options too, but these are sufficient to demonstrate that no contradiction exists here.

Was the Tomb Already Open When They Arrived?

Skeptics believe they have found yet another contradiction in these verses. According to these unbelievers, the Gospel writers disagreed about the tomb being opened or closed when the women arrived.

> Now after the Sabbath, as the first day of the week began to dawn, Mary Magdalene and the other Mary came to see the tomb. And behold, there was a great earthquake; for an angel of the Lord descended from heaven, and came and rolled back the stone from the door, and sat on it. His countenance was like lightning, and his clothing as white as snow. And the guards shook for fear of him, and became like dead men. (Matthew 28:1–4)

The other Gospels reveal that by the time the women arrived "they saw that the stone had been rolled away" (Mark 16:4; cf. Luke 24:2; John 20:1). So which is it? Did the angel roll away the stone before the women arrived or did they see him do it? Look closely again at Matthew's words. Notice that he does not claim that the women saw the angel do this. He tells us that the women set out to see the tomb, and then he mentions that an angel rolled the stone away and sat on it. There is nothing in Matthew's account that would preclude the angel performing these actions prior to the women's arrival at the tomb. In fact, it may be a safe assumption that the angel did this at or very near the moment of the Resurrection. As mentioned in chapter 4, the subtle detail that no one is said to have witnessed the actual event of the Resurrection lends credibility to the historicity of the account. The guards saw the angel, but Scripture does not tell us that they watched Jesus rise from the dead.

Another problem is raised by skeptics from these passages. Matthew is the only writer to mention the earthquake and the guards. Did he simply invent these details? The skeptic's anti-biblical bias is on full display here. Rather than giving the writers the benefit of the doubt, as we do with other authors, the skeptic assumes there is a contradiction involved because the other writers did not include particular details. It would only be a contradiction if Mark, Luke, or John claimed that an earthquake did not occur that morning and that there were never any guards at the tomb.

These divergent reports actually undermine one of the skeptics' claims about the Gospels. They often contend that the Gospels were written long after the time of Jesus by people who had never met Him. And that the early church leaders who allegedly wrote the Gospels were interested in strengthening their control over the growing Christian movement. Consequently, they condemned any writing that didn't fit their views and only promoted those works that bolstered their position. But the fact that so many minor differences (not actual contradictions) can be found in the Gospels shows that the early church leaders were not in collusion. They didn't get together and organize these accounts, making sure they all carried the same message. Instead, these slight variants between the Gospels support the Christian view that the books were indeed composed by the traditional authors who wrote what they witnessed or learned from those who did witness the events.

How Many Angels Were at the Tomb?

The Gospels also seem to contradict each other concerning the number of angels at the tomb that morning. Matthew mentions that an angel rolled the stone back from the door and sat on it. When the women arrived, the angel announced, "Do not be afraid, for I know that you seek Jesus who was crucified. He is not here; for He is risen, as He said. Come, see the place where the Lord lay" (Matthew 28:5–6).

Mark states that when the women entered the tomb "they saw a young man clothed in a long white robe sitting on the right side; and they were alarmed" (Mark 16:5). Luke mentions that while they were in the tomb, "two men stood by them in shining garments." John states that Mary Magdalene "saw two angels in white sitting, one at the head and the other at the feet, where the body of Jesus had lain" (John 20:11).

Two issues must be explained. First, why did Matthew and John describe these beings as angels when Mark and Luke called them men? The reason for this apparent disagreement is that when angels appeared to people in Scripture, they often appeared in human form, and were even occasionally called men.

In Genesis 17 and 18, two angels in the form of men left Abraham and traveled to Sodom to rescue Lot from that wicked city.

In Daniel 9:21, the prophet states that "the man Gabriel" came and revealed a remarkable prophecy to him. Those familiar with the Bible should recognize Gabriel as the angel who announced the birth of John the Baptist to Zacharias (Luke 1:19) and the virginal conception of Jesus to Mary (Luke 1:26). So it is perfectly acceptable for the Gospel writers to refer to angels as men when they appear in that form, as they obviously did in this case.

The number of angels described at the tomb varies within the accounts, but they do not contradict each other. Neither Matthew nor Mark claims that there was *only* one angel at the tomb. Matthew first describes the angel outside the tomb sitting on the stone. By the time the women arrive it is unclear from Matthew if the angel is still outside the tomb or inside it. Mark doesn't mention the angel being outside the tomb, but describes the "young man in a long white robe" inside the tomb sitting on the right side. His words are almost identical to what is recorded in Matthew. While there are other possibilities, it seems likely that Matthew's angel moved inside the tomb before speaking or spoke the same words twice. Luke has both angels in the tomb speaking to the women.

Once again, John seems to be at odds with the other accounts. He doesn't mention the appearance of any angels until Peter and John have already left the tomb, leaving Mary Magdalene weeping alone. She finally looks into the tomb and saw "two angels in white sitting, one at the head and the other at the feet, where the body of Jesus had lain." Since John refers to a later angelic appearance than in the other Gospels, there is no contradiction. Matthew, Mark, and Luke refer to when the women first arrived at the tomb, apparently without Mary Magdalene who seems to have turned back to get Peter and John as soon as she saw the opened tomb (see chapter 19). John describes an appearance of angels a little later that morning after the other women, Peter, and John had departed.

Conclusion

Many other examples of these minor discrepancies between the Gospel accounts could be explored, but these are sufficient to demonstrate that the accounts do not contradict one another. Differences in the accounts do not necessarily equal contradictions in the accounts. Four news reporters at the scene of a fire could have slightly different but non-contradictory reports too. So there is nothing unusual about differences in the gospel accounts.

Skeptics want to find contradictions in the text in their efforts to push out of their own minds the truth presented in these accounts: Jesus rose from the dead proving that He is indeed the Son of God who will one day judge the world. Rather than attacking the accurate historical records in a vain effort to justify unbelief, I urge these skeptics to turn from their sin and call out to the risen Savior for the forgiveness they so desperately need.

19 Are There Contradictions in the Order of Post-Resurrection Appearances?

The post-Resurrection appearances of Jesus have been discussed throughout this book as "infallible proofs" that Jesus rose from the dead, at least to those who saw Him. But skeptics have argued that the appearance accounts contain multiple contradictions, so they cannot be trusted. As I mentioned in the previous chapter, even if contradictions did exist in these accounts, it would not mean that He did not rise or that He did not appear to people after conquering death. However, it would mean that one or more of the Gospels were not copied accurately through the ages or that one or more of the writers made a mistake in their reporting of these events. But a reporting error about one or more of the minor details associated with the event does not prove that the event never happened.

If a legitimate contradiction existed in an original manuscript, it would undermine the doctrine of inerrancy, but it would not change the fact that Jesus rose from the dead and showed Himself alive by "many infallible proofs" (Acts. 1:3). The skeptic can never prove that a contradiction existed in the original autographs since these documents are no longer extant. Nevertheless, I do not believe there is any cause for concern since these accounts are demonstrably complementary rather than contradictory.

The skeptics have an obvious bias against the Bible being the Word of God. This is evident in their responses to Christian apologists who explain how these accounts are consistent with one another. The skeptics often do not look for a plausible explanation because they don't want to find one. They claim that we are guilty of special pleading when we provide legitimate solutions to the dilemmas they raise.

Sometimes I wonder if these same skeptics would act the same way if they were on trial for a crime they didn't commit. Would they want each of the defense witnesses shouted down and mocked when he provides a detail one of the other witnesses did not, or would they call the witness a fraud if she failed to mention a detail the other witnesses included? Of course not. The skeptic would want his attorney to explain to the jury how the eyewitness accounts fit together nicely, even though they did not contain all of the exact same details.

Telescoping

None of the Gospel accounts include all of the appearances Jesus made, so we must piece together data from the four Gospels and 1 Corinthians 15. Prior to considering all of these accounts, it is very important to understand that the Gospel writers often used a technique known as *telescoping* in their recounting of events. This means that in a person's reporting of events, he often strings several details together without indicating that gaps of time may exist in between the events he reports. This is a very common practice in secular historical writing, just as it is in the Gospels.

A classic example of telescoping in the Gospels is found as Jesus is sentenced and led out to be crucified. Luke stated that "Pilate gave sentence that it should be as they requested. And he released to them the one they requested, who for rebellion and murder had been thrown into prison; but he delivered Jesus to their will. Now as they led Him away, they laid hold of a certain man, Simon . . . " (Luke 23:24–26). If one had only read Luke's account of these matters, he may think that Jesus went straight from sentencing to being marched out to Calvary, but Matthew explains some details that Luke skipped over. Matthew reveals that after Pilate delivered Jesus to be crucified, the following occurred:

> Then the soldiers of the governor took Jesus into
> the Praetorium and gathered the whole garrison around
> Him. And they stripped Him and put a scarlet robe on
> Him. When they had twisted a crown of thorns, they put
> it on His head, and a reed in His right hand. And they
> bowed the knee before Him and mocked Him, saying,
> "Hail, King of the Jews!" Then they spat on Him, and
> took the reed and struck Him on the head. And when
> they had mocked Him, they took the robe off Him,
> put His own clothes on Him, and led Him away to be
> crucified. Now as they came out, they found a man of
> Cyrene, Simon by name. (Matthew 27:27–32)

That Luke neglected to mention these details does not mean he was unaware of them or that Matthew made them up. It simply means that for whatever reason, Luke chose not to report them. This is part of the nature of writing history. The historian selects which details he will include.

When it comes to the accounts of Christ's appearances, Luke frequently telescopes. If we only had access to the Gospel of Luke, it would seem like Jesus made all of His appearances in one day, but in his next book (Acts), Luke states that the Lord's appearances took place over a forty-day period. He was fully aware that all of the appearances were not on the same day, and he did not imply that they were in his Gospel—he just did not specify exactly when all of the appearances happened.

A Proposed Order of Appearances

Combining the information in the Gospel accounts can sometimes be a little tricky due to the number of partial reports and the amount of telescoping. All four Gospels assert that the women headed for the tomb very early in the morning. As they neared the tomb, they saw that it was already open.

Although not recorded by Matthew, Mark, or Luke, it seems that Mary Magdalene either decided herself or was selected by the others to turn back and notify Peter and John while the other women continued to the tomb. Upon arriving where Peter and John were staying, Mary exclaimed, "They have taken away the

Lord out of the tomb, and we do not know where they have laid
Him" (John 20:2). At this point, she apparently had no knowledge
of the angelic message. She seemed distraught that the Lord's
body was gone.

Meanwhile, the other women enter the tomb and see the
angels. Matthew reports that the angel told the women the
following:

> Do not be afraid, for I know that you seek Jesus who
> was crucified. He is not here; for He is risen, as He said.
> Come, see the place where the Lord lay. And go quickly
> and tell His disciples that He is risen from the dead, and
> indeed He is going before you into Galilee; there you will
> see Him. Behold, I have told you. (Matthew 28:5–7)

> The women left the tomb with a mixture of fear and
> great joy, and set out to inform the disciples of the angel's
> message. (Matthew 28:8)

Appearance #1: Mary Magdalene

As the women head back to the city, John, Peter, and Mary
Magdalene travel to the tomb. John outruns Peter, but Peter
enters the tomb first and sees the various grave cloths. John enters
the tomb, and he tells us that "he saw and believed" (John 20:8).[1]
Peter and John head back to their own homes, but Mary stays
behind at the tomb weeping. When she finally looks into the
tomb, she sees two angels who ask her why she is weeping
(John 20:13). After responding, she turned around and was given
a unique privilege. Thinking that a gardener stood before her, she
asked, "Sir, if You have carried Him away, tell me where You have
laid Him, and I will take Him away" (John 20:15). But this was no
gardener. Instead Mary Magdalene became the first eyewitness of
the mighty death-conquering Savior, Jesus Christ. He told her to
go and inform His brethren (John 20:17).

---

[1] Scholars are divided over whether John was claiming that he believed in the
Resurrection at this point, or if he was merely stating that he believed Mary's
report of the body being moved.

Appearance #2: The Other Women

The other women were still on their way back into the city or possibly to Bethany. Having heard the message of the angel, they were greatly afraid, and even though they were instructed to tell the disciples, it seems that they were scared to do so. Mark 16:8 states that "they said nothing to anyone, for they were afraid." But these dear women would soon meet the Savior. "Jesus met them, saying, 'Rejoice!' So they came and held Him by the feet and worshiped Him" (Matthew 28:9).

Appearance #3: Two Disciples on Road to Emmaus

After describing the initial visit to the tomb, Luke summarizes the details of that morning (Luke 24:8–12) without mentioning the appearances to the women.[2] He then proceeds to the third appearance. Later that day, Cleopas and another disciple were traveling from Jerusalem to Emmaus, roughly a seven-mile journey (Luke 24:13). Jesus came alongside them and talked with them on the way, yet they did not recognize Him (Mark 16:12). They were confused and saddened, having believed that Jesus "was going to redeem Israel" but instead He was crucified (Luke 24:20–21). They had heard reports of the women seeing angels and the report of Peter and John about the empty tomb, but had not heard of anyone seeing Jesus at that point (Luke 24:22–24). Upon arriving at their destination, Jesus broke bread with them.

---

[2] If Luke's summary in these verses is taken to be a complete report of the events, then we would have some problems, but there are good reasons to view these verses as an incomplete summary. "The only slight puzzle is Luke, who records neither encounter with Jesus. Two points need making here; firstly, Luke in his chronological account mentions neither the men's visit to the tomb nor the appearance to Peter himself - yet he clearly refers to both in later reported speech (Luke 24:24, 34) so it is obvious that Luke did not intend to imply that his report was complete. Secondly, there is no point in his narrative where he could insert either incident without spoiling the drama of realisation on the Emmaus road and the crescendo of the unmistakable appearance in Luke 24:36. Thus Luke 24:9-12 are a general summary, indicating the main characters and the general atmosphere of unbelief that prevailed. Both Mary Magdalene and the others *had* seen angels and *were* generally disbelieved, so what he actually says is true if incomplete." See "The Resurrection of Jesus: A Harmony of the Resurrection Accounts" available at < http://www.answering-islam.org/Andy/Resurrection/harmony.html>. Accessed February 8, 2014.

"Then their eyes were opened and they knew Him; and He vanished from their sight" (Luke 24:31). They quickly got up and headed back to Jerusalem.

Appearances #4 and #5: The Eleven Minus Thomas

Cleopas and his companion arrived in Jerusalem to find the eleven gathered together. This must have been one incredible meeting. Some of the disciples were excited, having heard reports that Jesus was alive again, while others still doubted (Mark 16:13). When Cleopas and his friend entered the house, they were told by some of the disciples, "The Lord is risen indeed, and has appeared to Simon!" (Luke 24:34). This matches Paul's statement that after rising from the dead, Jesus was seen by Cephas, the Aramaic version of Simon Peter's name (1 Corinthians 15:5). As they were discussing these events, "Jesus Himself stood in the midst of them, and said to them, 'Peace to you'" (Luke 24:36). Matthew is the only Gospel that does not include details of this meeting. The disciples who were present believed, but Thomas, who was absent, later infamously said, "Unless I see in His hands the print of the nails, and put my finger into the print of the nails, and put my hand into His side, I will not believe" (John 20:25).

Appearance #6: The Eleven

Thomas would not need to wait too long, although by missing out on something so exciting the following days likely seemed much longer to him. Eight days later, the disciples were together and Jesus came and stood in their midst. He said to Thomas, "Reach your finger here, and look at My hands; and reach your hand here, and put it into My side. Do not be unbelieving, but believing" (John 20:27). The response by Thomas is what I wish everyone would proclaim upon hearing the good news. Thomas said, "My Lord and my God!" (John 20:27).

The next few appearances may have occurred in a different order. We are simply not given enough details to know for sure when each of the following took place.

Appearance #7: The Seven in Galilee

Following the incredible events in Jerusalem throughout the long Passover festival, the disciples returned to Galilee. Seven of the disciples decided to go fishing at the Sea of Galilee, also called the Sea of Tiberias (John 21:1). They caught nothing during the night. In the morning, Jesus stood on the shore and instructed them to cast the net on the right side of the boat. They caught so many fish that they could not pull the net in. John surely recalled a similar miraculous catch of fish (Luke 5:4–7) and recognized that it was Jesus on the shore. When Peter heard that, he jumped into the water and swam to Jesus (John 21:7). It was during this appearance that Jesus restored Peter by asking him to affirm his love for Him three times, countering each of Peter's three denials on the night of Christ's arrest.

Appearance #8: The Mountain in Galilee

While the disciples were still in Galilee, Jesus appeared to them on the mountain which He "had appointed for them" (Matthew 28:16; cf. Matthew 28:7, 10). "When they saw Him, they worshiped Him; but some doubted" (Matthew 28:17). The disciples did not "doubt" that He had risen from the dead. They were fully aware that Jesus was alive, having seen Him multiple times already, but they were still unsure how to respond in His presence. See chapter 20 for a detailed look at the phrase, "but some doubted."

Appearance #9: The 500

It is possible that this appearance is the same event as the one mentioned previously. The Gospels never state that Jesus appeared to more than 500 people at once; this is found in Paul's writing (1 Corinthians 15:6). Many commentators believe this event took place on the mountain in Galilee. After all, His followers knew that He was going to appear to them in Galilee, so this is something they would have looked forward to. The Galilee hillside appearance is the only time where the witnesses knew ahead of time that He was going to appear. So it makes sense that there may have been a sizeable crowd. Nevertheless, Matthew is the only writer to mention the hillside event, so we have very few details to go on.

Appearance #10: James

The Gospels do not record the appearance of Jesus to James, so we cannot be sure about the details of what happened or when this occurred. We do know that James was an unbeliever at the time of the Crucifixion and by Pentecost he was a believer in the Upper Room with the other disciples. The only clue as to the timing of this event is found in 1 Corinthians 15. Paul mentioned the appearance to the 500 and then stated, "After that He was seen by James" (1 Corinthians 15:7).

Appearance #11: The Great Commission and Ascension

The disciples soon headed back to Jerusalem, perhaps at an unrecorded command of Jesus. They would have gone to Jerusalem a week later for the Feast of Pentecost, but for whatever reason, they were there 40 days after the Resurrection. After meeting them in Jerusalem, Jesus led them out to the Mt. of Olives "as far as Bethany" (Luke 24:50). During this time He gave them the Great Commission to make disciples of all nations (Matthew 28:18–20). He commanded them to remain in Jerusalem until the Holy Spirit came. "Now when He had spoken these things, while they watched, He was taken up, and a cloud received Him out of their sight" (Acts 1:9).

Appearance #12: Paul

Jesus still had one more appearance to make. This time it was for the purpose of turning the church's greatest persecutor into a tireless and faithful evangelist. The details and impact of the appearance to Paul were discussed in chapter 3.

Conclusion

There may be other possible ways to reconcile these accounts, and as mentioned earlier, some of the later appearances may have occurred in a different order. The purpose of this chapter was to show that the skeptical claim about contradictions in these reports is false.

We need to remember that partial reports are not necessarily false reports. We also need to keep in mind that it is perfectly acceptable for a writer to telescope certain events as he selects which details he is going to discuss and how to arrange them. The Gospel writers were inspired by God to provide an accurate record of the "infallible proofs" of the risen Savior. While the disciples and others were truly blessed with the privilege of seeing and touching Jesus after He rose from the dead, the words that He spoke to Thomas apply directly to believers today:

> Jesus said to him, "Thomas, because you have seen Me, you have believed. Blessed are those who have not seen and yet have believed." (John 20:29)

Are you among those who have not seen and yet have believed or have you still not bowed the knee to the Son of God? Do not wait until it is too late to call upon Him for salvation.

20 Did Witnesses Doubt Jesus Had Risen from the Dead?

Matthew 28:17 includes a strange phrase that has led to some confusion and generated some controversy. During Christ's post-Resurrection appearance on a hillside in Galilee, some of His disciples worshiped Him, "but some doubted." Critical scholars have sometimes used this phrase to support their idea that the disciples were only experiencing a vision.

Christians have disagreed over the right way to view this phrase. I have heard and read Christian apologists claim that these three words prove it is wrong to use evidence for the Resurrection in witnessing to unbelievers, even claiming that it would be sinful to do so. Others have taken nearly an opposite view. They use this phrase as evidence for the authenticity of the New Testament, because they believe Matthew included an embarrassing detail about some disciples not believing in Jesus even though He was right in front of them.[1]

What are we to make of these claims? How could people who knew Jesus had died on the Cross possibly not believe that He had risen from the dead when He was standing right in front of them?

Who Doubted?
First, let's take a look at the verses in question and cover a little background information.

---

[1] Geisler and Turek, *I Don't Have Enough Faith to Be an Atheist*, p. 231.

> Then the eleven disciples went away into Galilee, to the mountain which Jesus had appointed for them. When they saw Him they worshiped Him; but some doubted. (Matthew 28:16–17)

On the night of His arrest, Jesus told His disciples that He would rise from the dead and then meet them in Galilee (Matthew 26:32; cf. Matthew 28:10; Mark 16:7). The passage in question shows the fulfillment of that promise.

So the eleven disciples (the original twelve minus Judas who had hanged himself) went to a mountain or hillside (the Greek word *oros* can mean either one) in Galilee and when Jesus appeared to them, they worshiped Him, "but some doubted."

Who was doing the doubting? The context of this verse seems to show that it was some of the eleven disciples since no other people are mentioned here. As discussed in the previous chapter, many Christians believe this appearance on the hillside is where Jesus appeared to "over five hundred brethren at once" (1 Corinthians 15:6). There are at least two reasons why they make this connection. First, if only the eleven disciples were present, then it must have been some of those eleven disciples doing the doubting. However, this would be strange since all of them had already seen the risen Lord twice before, except Thomas who had only seen Him once as far as the Gospels inform us. They knew He had risen, so how could they doubt it? Second, there is a desire to connect the appearances in Paul's list with those in the Gospels. But the Gospels do not record the appearance to James (1 Corinthians 15:7), so maybe the appearance to over five hundred is not to be found in the Gospels either.

While I think it is possible that the Galilean hillside appearance was to over five hundred, there is no indication of this in Matthew's text. Sure, he could have left out information about the size of the crowd and simply focused on the eleven disciples. But even if it was only the disciples who were present, there is really no difficulty with the wording about doubt because the Greek term does not convey the same sort of doubt that most English speakers think of upon hearing that term.

A Big Misunderstanding

This is one of those cases where the English translation plays a role in the confusion. A careful look at the Greek term translated as "doubted" shows why all of the claims mentioned above are misplaced at this point.

The *doubt* exhibited here is not unbelief, but more like hesitation, which is what the Greek word διστάζω (*distazō*) implies.[2] Matthew did not use *diakrinō* here, which is the typical word for doubt found in the New Testament. *Distazō* is used only one other time in Scripture—Matthew 14:31, which will be discussed below. Instead of the disciples refusing to believe what they were seeing, as is often claimed, some of Christ's disciples were amazed. The concept here may be comparable to our modern statements like "It's too good to be true," or "Pinch me, I'm dreaming." Or given what Jesus had previously said in His first appearance to the group (John 20:21–23), they may have been concerned about how His command to go into the world would affect their lives

Craig Blomberg suggests other meanings of this "doubt" in his commentary on Matthew:

> *Distazō* refers more to hesitation than to unbelief. Perhaps, as elsewhere, something about Jesus' appearance makes him hard to recognize at first. Perhaps they fear how he may respond to them. Perhaps their Jewish scruples are still questioning the propriety of full-fledged worship of anyone but Yahweh. Or (most likely?) they may simply continue to exhibit an understandable confusion about how to behave in the presence of a supernaturally manifested, exalted, and holy being. There is no clear evidence that more than the Eleven were present, but the particular grammatical construction *hoi de* ("but some") does seem to imply a change of subject from the previous clause

---

[2] Walter Bauer, William F. Arndt, F. Wilbur Gingrich, and Frederick W. Danker, (*BDAG*) *A Greek-English Lexicon of the New Testament and Other Early Christian Literature*, 3rd ed., revised and edited by Frederick W. Danker (Chicago, IL: University of Chicago Press, 2001), s.v. "διστάζω," p. 252.

("they worshiped him"). So "they" probably means *some of the Eleven*, while "some" means *the rest of the eleven*. Some of the disciples worshiped Jesus at once; some were less sure how to react.[3]

Blomberg brings up some important points that most twenty-first century Christians would rarely consider. Yes, the disciples believed that Jesus was indeed God incarnate, as Thomas had recently acknowledged (John 20:28), but verbally admitting this was perhaps easier to do than fully committing oneself to worship Him. I agree with Blomberg that it is more likely that the disciples were still confused about how to behave in the presence of a supernatural being.

Think about Peter's behavior when he saw Jesus speaking with Moses and Elijah at the Transfiguration. While he was bold enough to speak up and clearly was trying to honor Jesus, Moses, and Elijah, it seems that he wasn't quite sure what to make of the event. As Moses and Elijah were departing, Peter said to Jesus, "Master, it is good for us to be here; and let us make three tabernacles: one for You, one for Moses, and one for Elijah" (Luke 9:33). Luke adds that Peter did not know what he was saying and reveals that he was quite sleepy (vv. 32–33).

What was wrong with Peter's statement? At first glance, it seems like he only wanted to prolong the experience; however, a closer look reveals that Peter may have been guilty of making a huge error. Robert Stein believes that Peter's mistake was that he wrongly placed Jesus on the same level with Moses and Elijah. However, "They were not equals. The Voice from heaven explains Peter's error. In contrast to Moses and Elijah, who were God's servants, Jesus is God's Son, the Chosen One. He is unique. He cannot be classed with anyone else, even two of God's greatest servants. He is not only great but other."[4] It might be easy for us to laugh at Peter at this point, but be honest, how would you respond if you witnessed the same thing?

[3] Craig Blomberg, *Matthew: The New American Commentary* (Nashville, TN: Broadman & Holman Publishers, 1992), p. 430.
[4] Robert H. Stein, *Luke: The New American Commentary* (Nashville, TN: Broadman & Holman Publishers, 1992), pp. 285–296.

Well, that's understandable before the Resurrection, but surely the disciples wouldn't act in a confused way after seeing Jesus alive again, would they? If only that were true. In the Bible's last chapter, John "fell down before the feet of the angel who showed" him the vision he had just seen. The angel essentially told him to stop it and worship God alone (Revelation 22:8–9). What's worse is that John had done the same thing and been similarly scolded just three chapters earlier (Revelation 19:10).

The point is that the disciples were overcome with emotion and still not sure what the unexpected and world-shattering events of the past few weeks meant when Jesus appeared to them in Galilee. And some of them were unsure how to react. They didn't know and understand what is so clear to us now with a completed New Testament and a worldwide Christian church. But they did not doubt that He had risen from the dead—they already knew this was true because they had seen Him in Jerusalem on Easter evening and eight days after that (John 20:19–29).

There are other passages that support this idea and show why the claims listed in the introduction to this chapter are illegitimate interpretations. Jesus appeared to the group of disciples (minus Thomas) on that first Easter night. Initially they were afraid, but He comforted them by showing them His hands and feet and telling them not to be afraid. Even after these things, we read that "they still did not believe for joy, and marveled" (Luke 24:41). The disciples already believed Jesus had risen from the dead, at least that's what they told the two disciples who had seen Jesus on the road to Emmaus: "The Lord is risen indeed, and has appeared to Simon!" (Luke 24:33–34). But now that they could see Him with their own eyes, they were amazed and rejoiced and yet their faith and joy were mingled with perplexities, which was the reason for their "doubt." And doesn't that happen to all Christians from time to time? We believe in and love Jesus Christ, but sometimes He "meets" us in some surprising circumstances and we struggle to respond appropriately.

Earlier in Christ's ministry, a man with a demon-possessed son pleaded with Jesus to cast out the demons. Jesus said, "If you can believe, all things are possible to him who believes." The man's response is intriguing—he cried out, "Lord, I believe; help my unbelief!" (Mark 9:14–24).

Finally, the only other place *distazō* appears in the New Testament is found in Matthew's account of Peter walking on the water. Peter had enough faith to get out of the boat and walk toward Jesus on the water. "But when he saw that the wind was boisterous, he was afraid; and beginning to sink he cried out, saying, 'Lord, save me!'" After Jesus rescued him, He asked, "O you of little faith, why did you doubt?" (Matthew 14:25–31).

In each of these cases, people exhibit faith in Christ's Resurrection or in His ability to perform a particular miracle. But at the same time, for whatever reason, they express some form of hesitation or doubt. Notice that none of these responses match what the critics claim. We don't see hardened skeptics standing there with arms crossed rejecting what is occurring before their eyes.[5] Nor do these instances line up with the Christian views mentioned in the introduction.

Moving Toward Faith

Once again, it is difficult for modern Christians to comprehend exactly what was going on here because we weren't part of the events. It would be wonderfully mind-blowing to have Jesus appear before us, and yet some of us have long believed that He rose from the dead. We haven't fathomed the depths of despair that Christ's followers experienced after His death. Most of us don't know what it was like to be a zealous monotheistic Jew trying to understand the nature and claims of Jesus of Nazareth and His mission in the world. None of us have had the opportunity to fully trust in Christ before He rose from the dead; we believe after the fact. That being the case, how can we possibly know the matchless exhilaration the disciples experienced when they saw Him alive again and yet had lingering doubts about what it all means? When we consider these things, it's quite simple to see why some of them thought it was too good to be true or weren't sure how to appropriately respond.

Gerald Borchert explained that in some of the post-Resurrection appearances we see that the people moving toward faith in Christ did not follow a set pattern. Commenting on Mary Magdalene's encounter with Jesus outside of the empty tomb, he wrote the following:

---

[5] Michael R. Licona, *The Resurrection of Jesus: A New Historiographical Approach* (Downers Grove, IL: IVP Academic, 2010), p. 360.

The transforming process of Mary coming to recognize the risen Lord took place when Jesus called her name, "Mary," or more precisely at this point "*Miriam*." It is fascinating to note that the Johannine evangelist has described transformative recognition occurring through the use of *one word* at this point. In the sea story it occurred when the disciples responded obediently to the stranger on the shore and cast their nets (in what seemed to be a foolish act) on the other side of the boat ([John] 21:6–7). In the Lukan Emmaus story the recognition occurred in the breaking of bread. What should be concluded from these examples is that recognition of Jesus does not need to follow a single pattern. Coming to the point of conviction that Jesus is alive is probably as varied as the nature of the people who believe.[6]

Conclusion

"But some doubted." These three words do not imply unbelief in the Resurrection on the part of the eyewitnesses. As such, this phrase does not support the idea that the disciples merely experienced visions of the risen Savior. Also, these words cannot be used to support the idea that it's wrong for Christians to discuss the evidence for the Resurrection while discussing the topic with unbelievers. The disciples knew full well that He had risen from the dead, but some of them were apparently unsure how to react in the wake of an astounding supernatural event that they did not yet know would change the course of history and turn the world upside down.

---

[6] Gerald L. Borchert, *John 12–21: The New American Commentary* (Nashville, TN: Broadman & Holman Publishers, 2002), p. 300.

21 How Was the Resurrection of Jesus Different from Others Raised from the Dead?

How can the Resurrection of Jesus be unique when there are many other people in Scripture that were raised from the dead? The word *resurrection* is a translation of the Greek word *anastasis*, which means to stand up or rise up, particularly in reference to one who has died. In this sense, the resurrections in Scripture are similar since they all have to do with a dead person being brought back to life. Let's take a tour through the Bible to see that the raising of the dead occurred on numerous occasions.

Old Testament Examples

The Son of the Widow of Zarephath

In 1 Kings 17:17–24 we read about a prophet named Elijah raising a widow's son from the dead. Elijah had been staying in Zarephath, in the house of the widow during a terrible drought, and God had provided for him, the widow, and the widow's son by miraculously giving her enough flour and oil for each day. After a while the boy became ill and died. Elijah "cried out to the LORD and said, 'O LORD my God, I pray, let this child's soul come back to him.' Then the LORD heard the voice of Elijah; and the soul of the child came back to him, and he revived" (vv. 21–22).

The Son of a Woman of Shunem

A similar account appears in 2 Kings 4:8–37, this time with Elijah's successor, Elisha. Elisha occasionally stayed in Shunem with a couple who had no children. Due to their hospitality for Elisha and his servant Gehazi, God provided the once-barren woman with a son. Sometime later the child complained of his head hurting and died shortly afterward. Elisha prayed over the dead child and twice stretched himself out on him, and the boy revived.

The Tomb of Elisha

Perhaps the strangest case of a person coming back to life occurred soon after Elisha's death. "Then Elisha died, and they buried him. And the raiding bands from Moab invaded the land in the spring of the year. So it was, as they were burying a man, that suddenly they spied a band of raiders; and they put the man in the tomb of Elisha; and when the man was let down and touched the bones of Elisha, he revived and stood on his feet" (2 Kings 13:20–21). There was nothing magical about the bones of Elisha. Rather this demonstrates that the power to raise the dead comes from God.

Jonah?

A possible revivification may have occurred in one of the Bible's most popular accounts. A prophet named Jonah was told to preach to the people of Nineveh, but he didn't want to go because he despised its inhabitants and wanted them to be judged. So Jonah tried to flee in the other direction, but a huge storm overtook the ship. Jonah believed the storm was due to his disobedience so he told the crew to throw him into the sea where he was subsequently swallowed by a great fish that God had prepared.

Most people assume that Jonah lived inside of the fish for three days, and he might have done that. But there are a couple of indications that he may have died during that time before God revived him. First, he spoke of crying out from the "belly of Sheol" (Jonah 2:2) and said that God had brought back his "life from the pit" (Jonah 2:6). *Sheol* and the *pit* are names for the abode of the dead. Also, in the New Testament, Jesus told some scribes and Pharisees that the only sign He would give them would be the "sign of the prophet Jonah. For as Jonah was three days and three nights in the belly of the great fish, so will the Son of Man be three days and three nights in the heart of the earth" (Matthew 12:39–40). As explained in chapter 15, Jesus truly was dead while He was in the "heart of the earth," so Jonah may very well have died too.

New Testament Examples

The Son of a Widow of Nain

The New Testament contains several reports of people being brought back from the dead. One day Jesus entered a city called Nain and he came across a funeral procession for a widow's only son. Jesus touched the open coffin and said, "Young man, I say to you, arise." The boy sat up and began to speak (Luke 7:11–15).

The Daughter of Jairus

In the Bible's next chapter we are told about a man named Jairus whose daughter was dying. He found Jesus and begged Him to come to his house to heal his daughter. While He was delayed by the crowds and the healing of a woman who had a bleeding problem, a messenger arrived to inform Jairus that the young girl had died. Jesus told the man not to be afraid and went to his house. He took the dead girl by the hand and said, "Little girl, arise." Immediately she arose, and Jesus instructed them to feed her (Luke 8:49–56).

Lazarus of Bethany

The Gospel of John records an extremely dramatic account of Jesus raising His friend Lazarus from the dead. After being informed that Lazarus was ill, Jesus delayed for a couple of days and Lazarus died. Jesus essentially told His disciples that He waited for Lazarus to die so that they would believe. When He arrived in Bethany, He spoke with Lazarus's sisters, Mary and Martha, and instructed some people to roll away the stone from the tomb. After a prayer, Jesus "cried with a loud voice, 'Lazarus, come forth!'" (John 11:43). Lazarus came out of the tomb, and many of the Jews believed in Jesus. Soon afterward, the chief priests plotted to kill Lazarus because he was a living testimony to the truth claims of Jesus and the power of God (John 12:10).

Interestingly enough, the reaction of the chief priests may have been predicted by Jesus in the well-known story that Jesus told about the rich man and Lazarus. In this tale, Lazarus was a poor beggar who died and joined Abraham in paradise. The rich man died and suffered the torments of Hades. The rich man begged Abraham to allow Lazarus to give him a drop of water. He pleaded with Abraham to send Lazarus back to his brothers and warn them about his agony in Hades so that they would not suffer the same fate. Then the following conversation took place:

> Abraham said to him, 'They have Moses and the prophets; let them hear them.' And he said, 'No, father Abraham; but if one goes to them from the dead, they will repent.' But he said to him, 'If they do not hear Moses and the prophets, neither will they be persuaded though one rise from the dead.' (Luke 16:29–30)

It is natural to think that Jesus used the words of Abraham in this story to allude to His upcoming Resurrection. But He may have had a different resurrection in mind when He claimed that the rich man's brothers would not be persuaded even if one were to rise from the dead. Is it merely a coincidence that Jesus used the name Lazarus in this story knowing full well He would soon raise His friend Lazarus from the dead and what the reaction of the people would be? Many Jews believed in Jesus upon seeing Lazarus alive again, but the chief priests not only continued to reject Jesus, they wanted to kill Lazarus to prevent even more people from believing in Jesus. These two responses fit Christ's words perfectly. Those who are willing to hear Moses and the prophets are open to believing in Jesus, while those who refuse to hear God's Word are unwilling to believe even when presented with such an incredible miracle. This was essentially the same reaction of the people when Jesus rose as well. Although when Lazarus was raised, some of the eyewitnesses ran back to report to the chief priests what had happened. These messengers apparently did not believe in Jesus at this point. There is no record of anyone in Scripture who remained in unbelief upon seeing the risen Jesus (see chapter 20 for an explanation of a common misunderstanding on this matter).

Many Saints at Christ's Death

A rather peculiar account of people raised from the dead is recorded only by Matthew. He wrote that soon after Jesus died on the Cross, the following events took place:

> Then, behold, the veil of the temple was torn in two from top to bottom; and the earth quaked, and the rocks were split, and the graves were opened; and many bodies of the saints who had fallen asleep were raised; and coming out of the graves after His resurrection, they went into the holy city and appeared to many. (Matthew 27:51–53)

These are the only details about this event provided in Scripture, and there are no surviving extra-biblical records of these matters. The Bible does not reveal how many people were raised from the dead at this point; it only tells us that "many bodies of the saints" were brought back to life.[1]

Tabitha

The book of Acts contains two accounts of someone being brought back to life. While Peter was in Lydda, a woman who "was full of good works and charitable deeds" passed away (Acts 9:36). Her name was Tabitha in Aramaic or Dorcas in Greek—both names mean *gazelle*—and she lived in nearby Joppa. Some believers sent for Peter and begged him to hurry. Peter arrived and knelt down before her body and said, "Tabitha, arise" (Acts 9:40), and her life was restored. Once again, the reaction of the people was similar to those who saw Lazarus or Jesus back from the dead. "And it became known throughout all Joppa, and many believed on the Lord" (Acts 9:42).

[1] This passage has been the occasion for no small controversy in recent years. Licona suggested that perhaps these verses were not meant to be understood as strictly historical. After noting various accounts of strange occurrences that followed the deaths of other important figures within a century of Christ's life, Licona proposed that Matthew's passage may be in a similar vein. In other words, rather than a reporting of literal events, Matthew used a "poetic device" as a way of announcing "that the Son of God had died and that impending judgment awaited Israel." Michael Licona, *The Resurrection of Jesus*, p. 553. Notable scholars have strongly criticized Licona for even raising this as a possibility, including Al Mohler and Norman Geisler. While I disagree with Licona's conclusion on this topic, he did raise some interesting points that I had never considered.

Eutychus

In a passage that has been lightheartedly used by some preachers as a warning against listeners falling asleep during the sermon, God performed a remarkable miracle through Paul. The apostle met with believers in Troas one Sunday. He continued to teach them until midnight, and a young man named Eutychus fell asleep while sitting in a window. He fell from the third story and died. Paul went down to where Eutychus lay dead on the ground and raised him back to life. After that, Paul continued speaking with them until daybreak (Acts 20:7–12).[2]

The Uniqueness of the Resurrection of Jesus

Each of these miracles is similar to the Resurrection of Jesus in that a dead person was raised to life. However, there are some notable differences. For example, the Lord's Resurrection was prophesied long before it actually happened. The Old Testament more than hinted at it (Psalm 16:10; cf. Acts 2:27; and Isaiah 53:8–10). Jesus specifically predicted it on numerous occasions (John 2:19; Matthew 12:40, 20:17–19).

Another huge difference has to do with the implications of the miracle. In the case of Jesus, the Son of God who willingly gave His life as a sacrifice for sin "was raised because of our justification" (Romans 4:25). If Jesus did not rise again, we could not be saved from our sin (1 Corinthians 15:14–19). In the other examples, normal human beings were brought back to life, but their miraculous resurrections carried no implications for our salvation.

Recognizing one of the major differences between Christ's Resurrection and the others mentioned in this chapter also answers the skeptical claim that Paul contradicted the other writers. In the great Resurrection chapter of 1 Corinthians 15,

---

[2] Many Christians believe Revelation 11 contains a prophecy of "two witnesses" who will be killed in Jerusalem and raised to life after three-and-a-half days (Revelation 11:1–14). Other than the discussion of the nature of our future resurrection bodies, the various eschatological views are beyond the scope of this book, so this passage is cited in a footnote as a possible prediction of a literal resurrection of two people. If this event is to be understood in this manner, then it would be similar to Christ's Resurrection in that these two individuals would not die again after being raised to life.

the apostle explained what will happen to those who die "in Christ."

> But now Christ is risen from the dead, and has become the firstfruits of those who have fallen asleep. For since by man came death, by Man also came the resurrection of the dead. For as in Adam all die, even so in Christ all shall be made alive. But each one in his own order: Christ the firstfruits, afterward those who are Christ's at His coming. (1 Corinthians 15:20–23)

How could Paul write that Jesus "has become the firstfruits of those who have fallen asleep" when so many others had been raised from the dead throughout Scripture? Was Paul simply unaware of these accounts? Certainly not. Paul was a brilliant student of the Old Testament, so he would have been quite familiar with the accounts mentioned above.

The main reason that Christ's Resurrection was different from these other individuals who were raised from the dead is that Jesus was the first to be raised in an incorruptible and immortal body. Each of the people mentioned above who were brought back from the dead eventually died again. Poor Lazarus not only died, but the chief priests wanted him to die again so that people would stop believing in Jesus on account of Lazarus (John 12:11), but even he would eventually die a second time, as would Tabitha, Eutychus, and the others.

Jesus was raised in an immortal body, giving us a glimpse of what awaits believers in the future. Paul elaborated on this future body at the end of the Resurrection chapter.

> Now this I say, brethren, that flesh and blood cannot inherit the kingdom of God; nor does corruption inherit incorruption. Behold, I tell you a mystery: We shall not all sleep, but we shall all be changed—in a moment, in the twinkling of an eye, at the last trumpet. For the trumpet shall sound, and the dead will be raised incorruptible, and we shall be changed. For this corruptible must put on incorruption, and this mortal must put on immortality. So when this corruptible has put on incorruption, and

this mortal has put on immortality, then shall be brought to pass the saying that is written:

Death is swallowed up in victory. O Death, where is your sting? O Hades, where is your victory?"

The sting of death is sin, and the strength of sin is the law. But thanks be to God, who gives us the victory through our Lord Jesus Christ. (1 Corinthians 15:50–57)

Not only did Jesus give us a glimpse of what our future bodies will be like, His conquering of death guaranteed that believers will also live again forever (John 3:16; Romans 8:11; 1 Thessalonians 4:14).

Conclusion

The Resurrection of Jesus is the most important miracle in history. Throughout Scripture, God displayed His power over death by raising certain individuals back to life. While these amazing miracles demonstrated God's power, they pale in comparison to the raising of Jesus from the dead, an event predicted long before it actually happened. The Lord's Resurrection was unique for numerous reasons: we could not be saved apart from it, He was raised in a glorified body, and His Resurrection guarantees our future glorification.

22 Is Easter a Pagan Holiday?

The notion that Easter is a pagan holiday may sound bizarre to many Bible-believing Christians who have celebrated the death, burial, and Resurrection of Jesus each year. What is even more curious is that some radical atheists and some conservative Christians find agreement in calling Easter a pagan holiday.

In an online article on the subject, one atheist writer made the following claim:

> The name of the holiday, "Easter," is the name of a pagan goddess that no decent Christian should be worshiping. A Christian theologian known as "The Venerable Bede" (672-735 CE) first identified this goddess as the origin of the holiday in his book De Ratione Temporum [sic]. The name "Easter" has a lot of variations (Ostare, Ostara, Ostern, Eostra, Eostre, Ester, Eastra, Eastur, Austron, Ausos, etc.) but all of these come from the same Roman goddess, the goddess of the dawn, named "Eos" or "Easter." Eos is the daughter of Hyperion and is the Greek equivalent of the Roman goddess Aurora.[1]

Several well-intentioned Christian writers have made very similar assertions. For example, concerning the supposed origins of Easter, David C. Pack described a Sunday family gathering

---

[1] Wm. Hopper, "An Atheist Easter: Origins and Myths" available at <http://heathensguide.com/04/23/an-atheists-easter-origins-and-myths>. Accessed on February 9, 2014.

complete with decorated eggs in seasonal baskets, hot cross buns, and a sunrise service, and then wrote the following:

> Easter, right? No! This is a description of an ancient Babylonian family—2,000 years before Christ—honoring the resurrection of their god, Tammuz, who was brought back from the underworld by his mother/wife, Ishtar (after whom the festival was named). As Ishtar was actually pronounced "Easter" in most Semitic dialects, it could be said that the event portrayed here is, in a sense, Easter. Of course, the occasion could easily have been a Phrygian family honoring Attis and Cybele, or perhaps a Phoenician family worshipping Adonis and Astarte. Also fitting the description well would be a heretic Israelite family honoring the Canaanite Baal and Ashtoreth. Or this depiction could just as easily represent any number of other immoral, pagan fertility celebrations of death and resurrection—including the modern Easter celebration as it has come to us through the Anglo-Saxon fertility rites of the goddess Eostre or Ostara. These are all the same festivals, separated only by time and culture.[2]

What are Christians to make of these charges? Are they accurate? Are the symbols, customs, name, and date of Easter truly of pagan origins? If so, are Christians who celebrate the Resurrection on that day guilty of pagan worship?[3]

The Symbols and Customs of Easter

Of all the claims made about Easter coming from pagan origins, the discussion about the symbols and customs is the only one that has any substantial support. When many people think of

[2] David C. Pack, "The True Origin of Easter" available at < http://rcg.org/books/ttooe.html>. Accessed on February 9, 2014.
[3] I am indebted to Roger Patterson for his excellent research on these topics. A few years ago, I asked him to write a series of articles on these topics for a series we were writing on misconceptions people have about the Bible and Christianity. His three articles are available at <www.answersingenesis.org> and are titled: "Is the Date of Easter of Pagan Origin?" "Is the Name 'Easter' of Pagan Origin?" and "Are the Symbols and Customs of Easter of Pagan Origin?" Much of this chapter will summarize his findings.

Easter, the immediate images that come to mind have to do with bunnies, candy, baskets, and eggs. If this is supposed to be a holiday dedicated to the Resurrection of Jesus, then what do these have to do with the risen Savior?

Few would deny that some pagan religions used eggs and bunnies as fertility symbols. The Catholic Encyclopedia acknowledges the pagan symbolism of these items. Regarding the bunny it states, "The rabbit is a pagan symbol and has always been an emblem of fertility."[4] Concerning eggs, the Catholic Encyclopedia states the following:

> Because the use of eggs was forbidden during Lent, they were brought to the table on Easter Day, coloured red to symbolize the Easter joy. This custom is found not only in the Latin but also in the Oriental Churches. The symbolic meaning of a new creation of mankind by Jesus risen from the dead was probably an invention of later times. The custom may have its origin in paganism, for a great many pagan customs, celebrating the return of spring, gravitated to Easter. The egg is the emblem of the germinating life of early spring.[5]

Nothing in Scripture links bunnies and eggs to the Resurrection of Jesus, and the use of these things as part of that celebration may well have been incorporated from pagan beliefs. However, this does not mean that Christians who color eggs and hide them for a children's hunt or give their children chocolate bunnies are guilty of worshiping pagan deities. Christians who use these things as part of their traditions are not viewing them as fertility symbols dedicated to false gods. Some Christians have even used the egg as a symbol of the Resurrection—from a seemingly dead object, new life springs. While the analogy is flawed, it can be a decent object lesson for children.

The period of Lent was mentioned in the quote above. This is a forty-day period of fasting recognized by the Roman Catholic Church and some Protestant denominations. Those who believe

---

[4] The Catholic Encyclopedia, "Easter," available online at <http://www.newadvent.org/cathen/05224d.htm>. Accessed February 9, 2014.
[5] Ibid.

Easter originated from pagan traditions often claim that this was adopted from a 40-day mourning period for Tammuz. One of the main problems for this view is that much of the information used to support it comes from Alexander Hislop's book, *The Two Babylons*, in which he attempted to link many of Rome's traditions to pagan practices. While there are undoubtedly links that can be made in some instances, Hislop often overstated his case or based his conclusions on shoddy information. Roger Patterson pointed out one of major oversights made by Hislop in his writings about Lent:

> Hislop cited the church historian Socrates of Constantinople, who suggested the customs are all regional and not of any apostolic origin. He also noted Cassianus, writing in the fifth century, who claimed the 40 days were not practiced in the "primitive Church." Hislop then concluded that the origin is from Babylonian worship and gave modern examples. This does not demonstrate the origin of the practice, only the coincidence of the practices. Hislop did not discuss the much earlier recognition of the period of 40 days of fasting noted by Irenaeus, so it seems his argument is based on incomplete information.[6]

Hislop's connection between Lent and Tammuz is dubious at best. After all, Irenaeus (d. AD 202) mentioned some Christians fasting for one, two, or even forty days—long before Rome supposedly borrowed it from the Babylonians.[7] But even if Hislop were correct that the tradition of Lent was adopted from the Babylonians, it does not follow that Christians who celebrate or fast for forty days prior to Easter are weeping for Tammuz. Many Christians may use this period of fasting to remind themselves of Christ's death, burial, and Resurrection, and there is certainly nothing pagan about that. Nor is there anything inherently pagan in fasting for forty days since Moses

[6] Roger Patterson, "Are the Symbols and Customs of Easter of Pagan Origin?" Available at <www.answersingenesis.org/articles/2011/04/26/symbols-easter-pagan>. Accessed on February 9, 2014.

[7] Irenaeus of Lyons, from a letter to Bishop Victor of Rome, in *Ante-Nicene Fathers*, vol. 1, ed. Alexander Roberts and James Donaldson (Peabody, Massachusetts: Hendrickson Publishers, 1994), pp. 568

(Exodus 34:28), Elijah (1 Kings 19:8), and Jesus (Matthew 4:2) did the same.

Furthermore, there is no basis for the claims that these other gods, like Tammuz, were resurrected from the dead. The notion that Christians copied the Resurrection from pagan gods was already refuted in chapter 8.

I have a question for those who are strongly opposed to any Christians celebrating Easter. Can a Christian celebrate Easter each year if he doesn't use any of these traditions that are allegedly linked with paganism? My family doesn't do the eggs and bunnies, and we've never set aside forty days prior to Easter for any special practices. Is it wrong for us to celebrate the Resurrection on the day called Easter? It may surprise some readers, but I've actually been told that it would still be wrong because the name of the holiday is pagan.

The Name of Easter

As mentioned earlier in this chapter, some people have alleged that the name "Easter" is taken from a pagan goddess who was worshiped in the spring. Once again, the main source for this claim is Hislop. A century after Hislop's book was published, Ralph Woodrow published *Babylon Mystery Religion* (1966) in which he drew heavily from Hislop. Woodrow later stopped circulating his early work and updated it in *The Babylon Connection?* (1997). In this work, he rejected many of Hislop's findings and pointed out the seriously flawed rationale that he used.

> By this method, one could take virtually anything and do the same—even the "golden arches" at McDonald's! The Encyclopedia Americana (article: "Arch") says the use of arches was known in Babylon as early as 2020 B.C. Since Babylon was called "the golden city" (Isa. 14:4), can there be any doubt about the origin of the golden arches? As silly as this is, this is the type of proof that has been offered over and over about pagan origins.[8]

[8] Ralph Woodrow, "Message form Ralph Woodrow Regarding the Book *Babylon Mystery Religion*," Ralph Woodrow Evangelistic Association. Available at <www.ralphwoodrow.org/books/pages/babylon-mystery.html>. Accessed February 9, 2014.

This is the same type of "logic" used by Hislop to associate the name "Easter" with the pagan goddesses known as Eostre, Astarte, Ashtoreth, Ishtar, etc. After all, the names look and might even sound similar, so they must be one and the same individual.

There is only one ancient source that mentions a goddess of the Saxons named Eostre. The church scholar known as the Venerable Bede wrote that one of the Saxons' months (Eosturmanath) was named after Eostre, a goddess who was celebrated with a feast in the spring. Bede's assertion was based on his "sketchy knowledge of other pagan festivals" and was part of a section of interpretations which Bede admitted were his own rather than generally agreed upon data.[9]

A much more compelling argument has been put forth that *Easter* comes not from Eostre but from an ancient Germanic language's word for *resurrection*.

> Because the English Anglo/Saxon language originally derived from the Germanic, there are many similarities between German and English. Many English writers have referred to the German language as the "Mother Tongue!" The English word Easter is of German/Saxon origin and not Babylonian as Alexander Hislop falsely claimed. The German equivalent is *Oster*. *Oster* (Ostern being the modern day equivalent) is related to *Ost* which means the rising of the sun, or simply in English, *east*. *Oster* comes from the old Teutonic form of *auferstehen* / *auferstehung*, which means *resurrection*, which in the older Teutonic form comes from two words, *Ester* meaning *first*, and *stehen* meaning to *stand*. These two words combine to form *erstehen* which is an old German form of *auferstehen*, the modern day German word for *resurrection*.[10] (emphasis in original)

---

[9] Anthony McRoy, "Was Easter Borrowed from a Pagan Holiday? The Historical Evidence Contradicts This Popular Notion." Available at <www.christianitytoday.com/ch/bytopic/holidays/easterborrowedholiday.html>. Accessed February 9, 2014.

[10] Nick Sayers, "Why We Should Not Passover Easter." Available at <www.easterau.com>. Accessed February 9, 2014.

This makes good sense since the name of this holiday in many other languages is based on their particular word for *resurrection* or their word for the Greek *pascha*, which is a transcription of the Hebrew word for Passover. Since the Resurrection was closely associated with the Passover festival, it is no wonder that the holiday celebrating the Lord's rising from the dead is named for *Passover* or *Resurrection*.

Those who think it would be wrong to celebrate the Resurrection on a holiday that may possibly be named after a pagan goddess have overlooked a crucial point. If Christians cannot celebrate holidays on a day named after false gods or goddesses, then we could never celebrate any holiday since some of our months and each of the days of our week are named after pagan deities. It's important to understand that Christians who celebrate the Resurrection of Jesus are worshiping Jesus on that day, not some pagan goddess whose name most have never heard.

The Date of Easter

Those opposed to the celebration of Easter have also alleged that the date is taken from the pagans as well. Many pagan religions had spring festivals, often on the vernal equinox, to celebrate new life and fertility. However, the date of Easter was clearly not chosen based on these dates. Church history is full of explanations for how the date of Easter was selected and it has nothing to do with pagan festivals.

The majority of the early church celebrated the Resurrection annually on the Sunday following Passover, since this is the day that Jesus rose from the dead. However, sometime during the second century, a group of Christians claimed that the Apostles John and Phillip established Nisan 14 (Passover) as the date of the festival. They became known as the Quartodecimans, which is Latin for the number "fourteen." For decades Christians peacefully disagreed on the matter, until Victor I (Bishop of Rome, AD 189–199) threatened to excommunicate the Quartodecimans near the close of the second century.

At the Council of Nicaea in 325, the church finally settled on a date that all could observe. They determined that the celebration would be held on the first Sunday following the first full moon after the vernal equinox. This would ensure that the celebration remained in the springtime, which is when Jesus rose. One of the concerns held by the bishops was that Passover had continued to move earlier in the year since the Jews used a different calendar. While I believe it to be a very poor reason, another rationale for unlinking the Resurrection celebration from the Passover was provided by Emperor Constantine:

> When the question relative to the sacred festival of Easter arose, it was universally thought that it would be convenient that all should keep the feast on one day; for what could be more beautiful and more desirable, than to see this festival, through which we receive the hope of immortality, celebrated by all with one accord, and in the same manner? It was declared to be particularly unworthy for this, the holiest of all festivals, to follow the custom [the calculation] of the Jews, who had soiled their hands with the most fearful of crimes, and whose minds were blinded....We ought not, therefore, to have anything in common with the Jews, for the Saviour has shown us another way....As, on the one hand, it is our duty not to have anything in common with the murderers of our Lord.[11]

Constantine's reason for changing the date was to distance Christian practices from Jewish practices since, in his view, Christians should not "have anything in common with the murderers of our Lord." This anti-Semitic statement is deplorable given the fact that Jesus and His apostles were Jews and first preached the gospel to the lost house of Israel. Also, all people, both Jew and Gentile, are guilty of sinning against God. Jesus said that He would be "betrayed to the chief priests and to the scribes; and they will condemn Him to death, and deliver Him to the Gentiles to mock and to scourge and to crucify. And the third day He will rise again" (Matthew 20:17–19). Constantine would have done well to recognize that Jews are not the only ones to blame

11 "On the Keeping of Easter," in *Nicene and Post-Nicene Fathers*, vol. 4, 2nd series, ed. Philip Schaff and Henry Wace (Peabody, Massachusetts: Hendrickson Publishers, 1994), p. 54.

for the Lord's death. Nevertheless, his disgraceful statement demonstrates that the date for Easter was not chosen to match some pagan celebration. Instead, it was selected to keep the holiday in the springtime and to disconnect it from the Jewish Passover.

But God Said...

Christians who think that their fellow believers must avoid these things often point to passages where God repeatedly prohibited Israel from serving other gods and following the practices of their pagan neighbors. For example, Deuteronomy 12 is full of God's commands to the Israelites forbidding them to worship foreign gods. Of course, I completely agree that Christians should never worship other gods. That is why on the day we call Easter (and every other day), my family and I worship the Lord Jesus Christ who died for our sins, was buried, and was raised from the dead.

The New Testament makes some very clear statements regarding the liberty that Christians have in this area. Paul stated, "So let no one judge you in food or in drink, or regarding a festival or a new moon or Sabbaths, which are a shadow of things to come, but the substance is of Christ" (Colossians 2:16–17). In this letter to the Colossians, Paul explained that godliness was not accomplished by one's philosophy, legalism, or asceticism. Instead, the requirements of the Law were nailed to the Cross, and we are to live by faith in Christ.

Paul wrote to the Romans about a similar issue. Since a large portion of the early church consisted of Jews, it was natural for the early church to wonder whether they should still be keeping the Sabbath and the other festivals. Paul's response was that Christians have liberty in these areas. Speaking particularly of the Sabbath, he wrote, "One person esteems one day above another; another esteems every day alike. Let each be fully convinced in his own mind. He who observes the day, observes it to the Lord; and he who does not observe the day, to the Lord he does not observe it" (Romans 14:5–6).

Christians have the freedom to keep the Sabbath or not to keep the Sabbath, but whichever choice is made, it should be done to the Lord. Likewise, we have the liberty to celebrate the Resurrection on Easter each year or not to do it. One should not be forced to violate his own conscience in these matters, and if a person decides to celebrate it, then celebrate it to the Lord. If a person decides not to celebrate it, then he should serve the Lord in whatever else he may do that day.

Only God's Festivals

Those Christians opposed to Easter have often been very outspoken against fellow believers for celebrating any holiday except for those festivals explicitly spelled out in the Old Testament. As such, anyone who celebrates Easter, Christmas, or some of the other Christian holidays have been attacked and accused of pagan worship.
These allegations often come from people caught up in what is called the Hebrew roots or Jewish roots movement. While their intentions may be to honor the Lord, their zeal is misplaced.

First, their actions are in some ways similar to the Judaizers who sought to add works of the Law, namely circumcision, to the gospel message. This would essentially turn the Christian faith into a works-based system, a teaching denounced in the strongest terms by Paul in Galatians 1:8–9.

Second, if they are correct that anyone who celebrates a holiday not spelled out in the Law is guilty of sinning, then they have created a very serious problem. Jesus may have celebrated Purim, and He apparently celebrated Hanukkah (John 10:22). If He did not celebrate it, He did travel to Jerusalem for it and the Gospels record no condemnation of the feast from the mouth of Jesus. As far as we know, God did not command the Jews to hold these festivals. The establishment of the holiday of Purim is found in Esther 9, which occurred roughly a thousand years after Moses was given the Law. Hanukkah was established to celebrate the rededication of the temple in 164 BC, following the Maccabean revolt against Antiochus IV Epiphanes. If it were truly sinful to celebrate a festival not spelled out in the Law, then why didn't Jesus point this out during the Hanukkah celebration? Why doesn't the New Testament prohibit Christians from celebrating the birth, death, or Resurrection of Jesus or the coming of the Holy Spirit at Pentecost?

Conclusion

Much more could be stated about each of these matters. This chapter only addressed some of the basics related to the celebration known as Easter. While some Christians have claimed that the customs, symbols, name, and date of Easter are of pagan origin, most of their assertions are without basis. Yes, some of the symbols have been used by pagans for the wrong reasons, but that would not prevent a Christian from using things such as eggs in a godly manner. God made eggs, bunnies, and everything else and pronounced them all "very good" originally (Genesis 1:31). Man is guilty of abusing these things, but there's no reason why they cannot be used in a way that glorifies Him.

But whatever Christians do on Easter or during Easter week, it should bring honor and glory to Christ. We should not do anything that would lead people (especially our children) to misunderstand what the celebration is all about: the death and Resurrection of Jesus Christ so that sinners could be restored to a right relationship with God and receive eternal life by repentance and faith in Jesus as Lord and Savior. The same principle would apply to any other "Christian" holiday. Of all times of the year, these are surely times when whatever we do in word or deed, we should do all in the name of the Lord Jesus, giving thanks through Him to God the Father (Colossians 3:17).

Furthermore, the name and date of the holiday do not have a pagan origin. However, even if it could be demonstrated that the Babylonians had an Easter celebration on the first Sunday after the first full moon following the vernal equinox to worship Tammuz, it would not make it sinful to worship Jesus Christ, the risen Savior, on that same day. He should be worshiped and celebrated every day of the year—on pagan holidays, Christian holidays, and even on days that are not considered holidays.

23 Do We Have a Hole in Our Gospel?

The first chapter of this book mentioned that the subject of the Resurrection is often overlooked in the church. This is indeed strange since Paul elaborated on the centrality of this doctrine in 1 Corinthians 15. Mathewson wrote, "Ironically, we often pay less attention to the resurrection than to the death of Christ. We glory in the cross of Christ, as we should (Gal. 6:14). But we give scant attention to the resurrection until Easter Sunday approaches."[1]

For the past several months I have paid close attention to the way many preachers and evangelists share the gospel, and I've been both saddened and shocked by the number of times the Resurrection is left out of the discussion entirely. I am not the only person to notice this disturbing trend. In his book, *Raised with Christ: How the Resurrection Changes Everything*, Warnock wrote about his own recognition of this development.

> I soon realized that [the] resurrection is not often discussed in detail. I found, however, that all of the sermons recorded in Acts focus on the resurrection of Jesus. It might initially seem like there is one exception in Acts 7, but in fact that sermon was interrupted when the risen Jesus himself opened heaven and appeared to Stephen while he was preaching! I was deeply struck by this, and realized that I had not given Jesus' resurrection the attention it deserved.[2]

[1] Mathewson, *Risen*, p. 12.
[2] Adrian Warnock, *Raised With Christ: How the Resurrection Changes Everything* (Wheaton, IL: Crossway, 2010), p. 21.

More than 150 years ago, Charles Spurgeon came to the realization that he had been neglecting this monumental doctrine.

> Reflecting, the other day, upon the sad state of the Churches at the present time, I was led to look back to Apostolic times and to consider wherein the preaching of the present day differed from the preaching of the Apostles. I remarked the vast difference in their style from the set and formal oratory of the present age. I remarked that the Apostles did not take a text when they preached, nor did they confine themselves to one subject, much less to any place of worship. But I find that they stood up in any place and declared from the fullness of their heart what they knew of Jesus Christ. But the main difference I observed was in the subject of their preaching. I was surprised when I discovered that the very staple of the preaching of the Apostles was the resurrection of the dead! I found myself to have been . . . leading the people of God as well as I was enabled, into the deep things of His Word. But I was surprised to find that I had not been copying the Apostolic fashion half as nearly as I might have done. The Apostles, when they preached, always testified concerning the Resurrection of Jesus and the consequent resurrection of the dead. It appears that the Alpha and the Omega of their Gospel was the testimony that Jesus Christ died and rose again from the dead according to the Scriptures. When they chose another Apostle in the place of Judas, who had become apostate, (Acts 1:22), they said, "One must be ordained to be a witness with us of His Resurrection," so that they very office of an Apostle was to be a witness of the Resurrection. And well did they fulfill their office![3]

If the Resurrection is a key component of the gospel, then are people really proclaiming the gospel when they fail to mention that Jesus rose from the dead? Is the gospel truly good news without the empty tomb?

[3] Charles Spurgeon, "The Resurrection of the Dead." A sermon delivered on February 17, 1856 at New Park Street Chapel, Southwark. Available at <http://www.spurgeongems.org/vols1-3/chs66-67.pdf>. Accessed February 17, 2014.

A Hole in the Gospel?

In 2009, Richard Stearns, CEO of World Vision, published a book titled *The Hole in Our Gospel: What Does God Expect of Us?* Stearns stressed the importance of putting the Christian faith into action, particularly as it relates to caring for the poor and downtrodden around the world. For Stearns, the "hole" in the Gospel for many Christians is that most American believers think that Christianity is primarily about a personal relationship with God, and they neglect a public relationship with the world designed to transform the culture.

While there are many important reminders in Stearns' book, he also makes numerous theological errors and drifts into the message of the "social gospel." This is a popular message among theological liberals. Rather than discussing the gospel as "the power of God to salvation for everyone who believes" (Romans 1:16), these individuals speak about the gospel as though it was meant to bring so-called "social justice" and the redistribution of wealth.

Popular pastor and blogger, Kevin DeYoung was asked to write a review of Stearns' book. In his critique, DeYoung acknowledged that Stearns' book had many strengths, and then he highlighted some of its problems. For example, DeYoung states, "I can't count all the times in the book we are told to change the world, start a social revolution, or usher in the kingdom of God. If only we gave more or had the will, we could eradicate hunger and win the war on poverty."[4] DeYoung responds by paraphrasing Paul's description in 1 Corinthians 15 of the gospel he preached: the death, burial, and Resurrection of Jesus. After making several more significant points, DeYoung closes his review with the following words:

> We must use words if we are to preach the gospel, because the gospel is a message we must proclaim. If we never live like Christians, we are not Christians. But to tell people that they must repent and believe in Jesus for the remission of sins, to tell them that God sent His

[4] Kevin DeYoung, "A Hole in Our Gospel?" Available at <http://thegospelcoalition.org/blogs/kevindeyoung/2010/06/15/a-hole-in-our-gospel>

Son in love to bear His just wrath, to tell them that they must receive the kingdom in faith like little children, *is not a gospel with a hole in it.* It is precisely the center, and Stearns's call to action would have been more compelling if it more clearly radiated from there. (emphasis added)

I appreciate DeYoung's review and believe he is right to emphasize the points he did. However, did you notice what he missed in his closing remarks? His description of the gospel at the end of his article is actually a "gospel with a hole in it." By this point in the book you should be able to figure out what he forgot to mention in summarizing the gospel: the Resurrection!

Something's Missing

The previous example is not intended to single out Pastor DeYoung. As stated above, earlier in the article he did mention that the Resurrection is part of the gospel message, but sadly, far too many Christians forget to mention this foundational element of the good news when witnessing to people. The more attention I pay to the Resurrection, the more I notice that Christians often overlook it.

I recently spoke with a friend about this troubling development. Here's a paraphrase of how I started our conversation. "Tell me if this is an example of sharing the gospel. We have all sinned against God and are separated from Him because of our sin. We deserve death and eternal separation from Him because of our rebellion. But the good news is that God's Son, Jesus, became a man, and He died on the Cross as a sacrifice for our sins. All those who turn from their sin (repent) and believe in Him will be saved."

My friend thought about it for a few moments and then said he thought that was an example of the gospel being presented. But did you notice what I left out? I never mentioned the Resurrection. When I explained that to my friend, his response perfectly made my point. He said that he thought that a lot of people probably just think about verses like the one in Romans that says if you believe in Jesus and confess Him as Lord, then you will be saved. Why was this a perfect response to make my point? Here is the verse he referred to:

...that if you confess with your mouth the Lord Jesus and believe in your heart *that God has raised Him from the dead*, you will be saved. (Romans 10:9, emphasis added)

In trying to make his point about why people might leave the Resurrection out of the discussion, my friend wrongly paraphrased Romans 10:9 by leaving the Resurrection out of it. Needless to say, he was slightly embarrassed when I showed him the verse and what he had missed.

I believe my friend was on to something, at least in some cases. Surely, many Christians have unintentionally forgotten to mention the Resurrection while sharing their faith. Perhaps they focus on a verse like John 3:16, which we often say is a good summary of the gospel—and it is in a sense. Jesus spoke these words prior to His death, burial, and Resurrection, explaining to Nicodemus that belief in God's Son will bring everlasting life. But the rest of John's Gospel (and the other Gospels) flesh out some critical details about God's Son. He came to die on the Cross for our sins and then conquer death by rising from the dead. The gospel isn't the good news only because Jesus died for our sins; it is good news because He died for our sins *and* He conquered death, which allows Him to perform His present and future ministries and give us resurrection life now and for eternity (Romans 6:1–11).

Why Is There a Hole?

Why do so many people forget to mention the Resurrection when talking about the gospel? Obviously, liberal theologians avoid the topic because they don't believe that Jesus physically rose. But for Bible-believing Christians, in addition to the unintentional oversight mentioned above, I believe there are several reasons why people leave this gaping hole in their gospel presentation.

First, many genuine Christians are so focused on what Jesus did for us on the Cross that it overshadows what happened three days later. Praise God that they focus on the Cross and all that Jesus accomplished, but that's only part of the good news. It is mind-blowing to think that the Creator of the universe, the Son of God, became a man to die in our place on the Cross, satisfying the righteous justice of the Father so that we can be forgiven. How could we not emphasize these glorious truths? Yet, if we forget to mention the Resurrection, how is the message of the Cross good news? If we only tell people about the Cross, where is the victory over death? Does our hope of eternal life remain buried in the tomb as well?

To be fair to individuals like this, I believe many Christians think of the Crucifixion and Resurrection as one big event, so when they discuss the Cross, in their minds, the Resurrection is a given as well. We have to constantly remind ourselves that unbelievers do not think this way, and they need to be told not only about Christ's atoning sacrifice on the Cross, but also about the death-conquering Savior rising from the tomb.

The second reason the Resurrection is neglected by some Christians is related to the first. Some believers get so caught up in debating various aspects of the Cross that they forget to mention what happened next. Was Jesus crucified on a Wednesday, Thursday, or Friday? Did He die for all people or only for the elect? Were the nails driven through His palms or wrists? There is nothing wrong with trying to figure out the answers to these questions, but some people get so fixated on these issues and others like them that they forget to explain that the same Jesus who died on the Cross rose from the dead a few days later.

Third, I believe some Christians neglect to mention the Resurrection because, in some ways, they shy away from discussing miracles. I am not claiming that they don't believe in miracles, but for some reason, they would rather not talk about God's miraculous intervention in our world. Telling people that Jesus died on the Cross is easier for them since everyone knows that people have been crucified before. There is nothing miraculous in executing a person. Of course, the Crucifixion of Jesus is not just about Him dying, but also about the reason that He died—as a sacrifice for our sins. But this transaction of our sins being forgiven as a result of Christ's death is something that can only be taken by faith.

On the other hand, to discuss the Resurrection with an unbeliever means that we must take the time to explain that the omnipotent God raised His Son back to life in this physical world. One of the greatest miracles occurred outside of Jerusalem in a garden tomb nearly 2,000 years ago: Jesus Christ conquered the grave and showed Himself alive by "many infallible proofs" to over 500 people. For whatever reason, some believers are uncomfortable discussing this truth, even though they believe it really happened.

A fourth reason that some people neglect the Resurrection when explaining the gospel was described in the first chapter. It is what I call the "Passion Syndrome." In Mel Gibson's film, *The Passion of the Christ,* viewers are shown approximately two hours of vivid, gut-wrenching torture endured by Jesus. The film ends with a little more than one minute depicting the Resurrection. Yes, it is important to understand what Jesus went through for us, although no film could ever capture the level of emotional and spiritual agony Jesus suffered for us when the sinless Lamb of God was made a sin offering for us (2 Corinthians 5:21). Watching the physical torment He experienced is very moving and emotionally gripping. Consequently, some believers attempt to use the sufferings of Christ in a way that may lead the unbeliever into responding to the message out of emotion.

Certainly one's response to the Savior should be emotional in some way, although it will vary from person to person. When a sinner realizes that the Son of God loved us so much that He was willing to suffer all the brutality man could dish out and then die on the Cross, it should touch our emotions. However, turning from sin and giving one's life to the Savior should not be done purely out of emotion. It should also involve one's intellect and will. Sinners need to understand that the message they are committing to calls us to die to self and live wholeheartedly for Jesus Christ (Luke 9:23–26, 14:25–33). And they need to hear that Jesus not only suffered and died, but He also rose from the grave, and "is able to save to the uttermost those who come to God through Him, since He always lives to make intercession for them" (Hebrews 7:25).

Of First Importance

Look once again at Paul's words to the Corinthians at the opening of the Resurrection chapter.

> Now I make known to you, brethren, the gospel which I preached to you, which also you received, in which also you stand, by which also you are saved, if you hold fast the word which I preached to you, unless you believed in vain. For I delivered to you *as of first importance* what I also received, that Christ died for our sins according to the Scriptures, and that He was buried, and that He was raised on the third day according to the Scriptures, and that He appeared to Cephas [Peter], then to the twelve. (1 Corinthians 15:1–5, NASB, emphasis added)

Paul reminded the Corinthians of the gospel message he preached to them, and by which they were saved. He said that this message was "of first importance." What was this message that was of primary concern? Paul preached that Jesus died for our sins, was buried, and was raised from the dead on the third day according to the Scriptures.

This fits well with the rest of Paul's letters since he refers to the Resurrection fifty-three times throughout his letters, often asserting the primacy of the Resurrection or the assurance it gives us of our own future.[5]

In the first chapter, I briefly explained how important the Resurrection is to the Christian faith and how central it was to apostolic preaching. In fact, it is impossible to overstate just how vital the Resurrection is to Christianity and all of life. A recent book on the subject rightly asserts the following bold claims:

> To say that Jesus, his early apostles and the Christian church have placed significant emphasis on Jesus' resurrection is to put it mildly. Everything Jesus taught and lived for depended upon his death and resurrection. All the promises and prophecies in the Bible depend on the resurrection. The whole history of God's plan to

---

[5]   Josh McDowell and Sean McDowell, *Evidence for the Resurrection: What It Means for Your Relationship with God* (Ventura, CA: Regal, 2009), p. 52.

restore his relationship with man and woman depends on the resurrection. It is not overstating the facts at all to say that the resurrection of Jesus is the single most important event in the history of the world. Your life and mine depend on the resurrection.[6]

Amen. May we all strive to remember the centrality of the Resurrection at all times so that there is never a hole in our proclamation of the gospel message.

[6] Ibid., p. 53.

24 What Does Genesis Have to Do with the Resurrection?

While the Lord originally called all creation "very good" (Genesis 1:31), He seems to have a special affinity for certain people and places. For example, He apparently holds a special place in His heart for shepherds. David, a man after God's own heart (1 Samuel 13:14), was a shepherd early in his life. He wrote the famous words, "The LORD is my Shepherd," which Jesus likely had in mind when He declared that He is "the good shepherd" (John 10:11). Of all possible occupations, it was lowly shepherds to whom the angel appeared and announced "good tidings of great joy" when Jesus was born (Luke 2:8–14).

The Bible frequently uses the shepherd as a picture of God (Isaiah 40:11; Zechariah 13:7; Hebrews 13:20) or the leader(s) of His people (Zechariah 10:3; Acts 20:28; 1 Peter 5:2). His followers are often compared to sheep (Jeremiah 23:1; Ezekiel 34:6; John 10:11–16; Acts 20:28; 1 Peter 5:2), while those who seek to harm His people are called wolves (Matthew 7:15, 10:16; Acts 20:29).

The Garden of Gethsemane

Similarly, it seems that God has an affinity for gardens, as three of the most important events in human history occurred in these places. On the night of His arrest, Jesus led His followers to the Garden of Gethsemane on the Mount of Olives where He poured out His soul to the Father in prayer (Matthew 26:36–46). He pleaded for the protection and unity of His immediate disciples and for all of us who would come to faith through their ministry (John 17:15–23).

Perhaps most significant is that it was also during this time in the garden that Jesus affirmed His commitment to carry out the plan of redemption—no matter how agonizing it would be.

> He knelt down and prayed, saying, "Father, if it is Your will, take this cup away from Me; nevertheless not My will, but Yours, be done." Then an angel appeared to Him from heaven, strengthening Him. And being in agony, He prayed more earnestly. Then His sweat became like great drops of blood falling down to the ground. (Luke 22:41–44)

Even though Jesus was "sorrowful and deeply distressed" (Matthew 26:38), He completely submitted Himself to the Father's will. After a period of intense prayer, Jesus went out to meet the great multitude that had come to arrest Him. He was determined to "endure the cross" and ready to despise its shame (Hebrews 12:2).

The Tomb in the Garden

All four Gospels record the burial of Jesus in the tomb of Joseph of Arimathea. John records the following details:

> Now in the place where He was crucified there was a garden, and in the garden a new tomb in which no one had yet been laid. So there they laid Jesus, because of the Jews' Preparation Day, for the tomb was nearby. (John 19:41–42)

A few days later, Jesus gloriously conquered death by rising from the dead in that garden. Early in the morning, while it was still dark, at least five women set out with spices to visit the tomb in which Jesus had been buried (Luke 24:1, 8). When they arrived, they discovered that the massive stone had been rolled away from the opening of the tomb and that the body was no longer in the tomb.

After informing the disciples of these things, Mary Magdalene returned to the tomb where she would become the first witness of the resurrected Savior. At first glance, she thought Jesus was the gardener and said to him, "Sir, if You have carried Him away, tell me where You have laid Him, and I will take Him away" (John 20:15). The fact that she thought He was a gardener reiterates John's earlier statement that the tomb was in a garden.

Is there any special significance that these two critical events in the ministry of Jesus took place in gardens? Perhaps not, but it is interesting that these events were set in motion 4,000 years earlier in another garden. In fact, Jesus came to earth, died on the Cross, was buried in a tomb, and rose from the dead because our first parents rebelled against God in the Garden of Eden.

The Garden of Eden

"Very good." That is how God described the original creation upon its completion (Genesis 1:31). There was no death, sin, bloodshed, or disease in this unspoiled environment. That all changed when Adam and Eve rebelled by eating from the tree of the knowledge of good and evil (Genesis 3:6–7), shattering the perfection of this world.[1]

God had already told Adam that the penalty of violating His command was death (Genesis 2:17). The Lord would have been entirely justified in carrying out this sentence immediately—after all, the holy Creator must punish rebellion or He would not be just. But God is also loving, merciful, and gracious. Adam and Eve would still physically die, but the Lord delayed the ultimate execution of their sentence.

---

[1] Some people object to describing the original creation as perfect since it was eventually corrupted. However, like many other words, *perfect* has multiple meanings. The first definition of the term in *Merriam-Webster's* is "being entirely without fault or defect." We often use it this way when speaking of an undefeated sports team at a certain point in their season. Their record is without blemish, but it does not mean that they are incapable of losing, and most eventually do lose, at which point they are no longer perfect. The king of Tyre (Satan may also be in view here) is described this way in Scripture: "You were *perfect* in your ways from the day you were created, till iniquity was found in you" (Ezekiel 28:15, emphasis added). The third meaning of perfect in *Merriam-Webster's* refers to someone or something that is "Pure, total," and "lacking in no essential detail: complete." This is often how we use the term when speaking of God. He is morally perfect, incapable of being corrupted. So those who object to describing the original creation as perfect are committing the fallacy of equivocation by confusing two of the ways this term can be used. Frederick C. Mish, Editor in Chief, *Merriam-Webster's Collegiate Dictionary*, 11th ed. (Springfield, MA: Merriam-Webster, 2008), s.v. "Perfect."

In place of the fig-leaf coverings Adam and Eve had made for themselves, "the LORD God made tunics of skin, and clothed them" (Genesis 3:21). These words imply that God must have killed at least one animal to make these garments, giving our first parents a vivid illustration of the devastation of sin. Man's sin brought death and corrupted this world (Romans 5:12, 8:22; 1 Corinthians 15:21). No longer would Adam and Eve enjoy a flawless environment. Instead, among other things, childbirth pains would intensify and man's labor would become toilsome and less efficient as thorns and thistles would infest the ground—the ground to which man would ultimately return in death.

The death of that first animal also provided a lucid picture of sacrifice, foreshadowing what God Himself would ultimately do through Jesus Christ, the "Lamb of God," to rescue sinners from the eternal consequences of their sin. In the years following that first sacrifice, other sacrifices for sin were offered to God by righteous men like Abel (Genesis 4:4), Noah (Genesis 8:20), Abraham (Genesis 22:13), and Job (Job 1:5). In the days of Moses, God gave more detailed instructions regarding sacrifices, and over the centuries the Levitical priests sacrificed millions of animals to the Lord.

The Gardens Are Linked

Whether these people realized it or not, their sacrifices all pointed forward to the greatest sacrifice of all. God Himself became a descendant of Adam, taking on human flesh and being born of a virgin, so that He could offer Himself as the final, once-for-all sacrifice (Hebrews 7:27). Jesus, the spotless and sinless Lamb of God, bore the sins of the world and endured the wrath of God upon Himself as He hung on the Cross. His death satisfied God's justice, but that wasn't the end of the plan. Three days later, in fulfillment of His promises (Matthew 20:17–19; John 2:19), Jesus victoriously rose from the grave, demonstrating His power over sin and death and guaranteeing our hope of eternal life with Him.

Man's rebellion in the garden brought death and suffering into this world that would eventually be conquered by the glorious Resurrection of Jesus Christ in a garden. Sadly, many

Christians fail to recognize the importance of the events in the first garden. In doing so, they relegate these events to the realm of myth, allegory, or symbolic poetry. Some have even claimed that Adam never existed, and many others have argued that death and suffering have been around for billions of years, meaning that these things are here because God made the world that way and still called it "very good."

This idea strikes at God's perfectly good nature and raises a crucial theological problem. If Adam's sin did not bring death into this world, then why would the death of Jesus, "the last Adam" (1 Corinthians 15:45), have anything to do with our sin? Why would Jesus need to become a man to physically die for sin if physical death was not brought into the world by man? What possible connection would there be between the death of the Savior and man's sin if man's rebellion was not the cause of death? And why would the last Adam need to physically rise from the dead to defeat sin and death if physical death had nothing to do with sin?

Without Adam's sin in the Garden of Eden, there would be no reason for Jesus to agonize in the Garden of Gethsemane over the mental, spiritual, and physical torment He would soon undergo in our place. And without these events, there would be no glorious Resurrection of the last Adam in the garden near Calvary. By reinterpreting the early chapters of Genesis to accommodate evolution and millions of years, these Christians unintentionally undermine the message of the Crucifixion and Resurrection of Jesus by removing the history in which these events are rooted.

Conclusion

Jesus gave His followers "infallible proofs" that He had risen from the dead (Acts 1:3). God has also given us infallible proof that He created a perfect world, which we subsequently wrecked through our sin. He has revealed these things to us in His infallible Word, the Bible. Just as we can have complete confidence in the Resurrection of Jesus Christ in the garden near Calvary, we can rest assured that the events in the Garden of Eden also happened, as described in Genesis 1–3.

God may indeed have a special affinity for shepherds and gardens, but He also has an extraordinary love for each human being, whom He created in His image (Genesis 1:26–27). The Good Shepherd told Nicodemus, "For God so loved the world that He gave His only begotten Son, that whoever believes in Him should not perish but have everlasting life" (John 3:16).

The bad news is that we have all sinned and fallen short of the glory of God (Romans 3:23), and the wages of our sin is death (Romans 6:23), just as God told Adam in the Garden (Genesis 2:17). But the good news is that the Good Shepherd willingly gave His life to redeem us from our sin. Jesus Christ offers complete forgiveness and eternal life to all who will turn from their sin (repent) and place their faith in Him, the all-sufficient, glorious, eternal, and risen Lord and Savior. If you have not done so already, would you call on the name of the Lord and be saved (Romans 10:9–10, 13)?

25 How Can the Resurrection Be a Source of Comfort?

Much of this book has consisted of arguments demonstrating the truth of the Resurrection of Jesus as an event that actually occurred in space and time nearly two thousand years ago. There has also been much discussion concerning theological matters related to this key doctrine. To me, these issues are deeply practical for many reasons. For example, Jesus rising from the dead demonstrates the truthfulness of His claims, His supernatural ability to accurately predict the future, and His power over death. Since Jesus affirmed the teachings of the Old Testament during His ministry, then we can have absolute confidence in the truthfulness of those writings.

The practicality of the doctrine of the Resurrection is not readily apparent to some people, so this chapter will focus on one issue that is of major concern to nearly every person. How can the Resurrection of Jesus help me in the here and now? Is belief in the Resurrection only about my eternal salvation (as if that wouldn't be enough), or is there more to it than that?

Death Is Not the End

Monday evening, July 17, 2006. "If I fall asleep, I'm not going to wake up." Those were the words I spoke to my wife as I lay in the Intensive Care Unit fighting against the leukemia that had silently taken over my body. I was saying goodbye to her, and to my mother who sat on the other side of my bed. I didn't know what would happen to me physically over the next few hours, days, or weeks. What I did know is that I was in extremely rough shape and my life was hanging in the balance.

But I knew something else beyond any shadow of a doubt— something that brought me tremendous peace during the hour of my greatest need.[1] I knew that if I lost my battle with leukemia that night or in any of the days to come, my goodbye was only temporary. Because God raised Jesus from the dead, He "will also raise us up" (2 Corinthians 4:14). For the Christian, death is not the end—it's graduation day. It's when we finally move on to our true home, to eternal life with our Creator, and there will be no more sorrow, pain, suffering, or death.

These truths can be exceedingly comforting to the person who is facing trials, suffering, or even death. Thanks to the Resurrection, I could face those troublesome hours with confidence and peace of mind. But what about my family? How could the Resurrection provide comfort to two kids who were facing the loss of their father? What hope could the Resurrection give to my wife while she wondered if she would soon bury me or to my mother who watched her son fight for his life? Does Christ's victory over death offer any comfort to those who grieve the loss of a loved one?

Dr. Gary Habermas is widely recognized as one of the world's leading authorities on the Resurrection, but he also knows tremendous grief. In 1995, his wife Debbie was diagnosed with stomach cancer, and just four months later, shortly after their 23rd wedding anniversary, she was gone. Habermas wrote the following about his grief:

> I had lost my best friend. All four of our children lived at home, and witnessing their pain was painful to me. Did they have to suffer like this? Would they have lasting scars from watching their mom die? Would they blame God? I was suffering a double dose of grief. I often thought that I could not have experienced pain any worse than this.

---

[1] To learn more about the lessons I learned during my leukemia battle and how one can trust in God's goodness even during life's most difficult challenges, see my book, God and Cancer: Finding Hope in the Midst of Life's Trials. Available at www.midwestapologetics.org/shop.

I knew that the resurrection had a historical, theoretical side, but I wasn't fully aware of its practical power. I had much to learn about applying Jesus' resurrection to my daily life.[2]

Theologically and philosophically minded people desire to have answers for every question. We want to figure out why things are the way they are and satisfy our own curiosities about life's difficult issues. But in times of immense sorrow and suffering, our having the right answers doesn't always satisfy, and it doesn't necessarily make the pain go away. Habermas also wrote about the tremendous suffering Job endured and imagined having a similar conversation with the Lord concerning his own grief and pain.

> "Lord, I just do not understand why You are allowing these things to occur to my family. Why, especially when Debbie is so young, and all four kids are still at home?"
>
> "Gary, I will answer your question with one of My own. Did I raise My Son from the dead?"
>
> "Well, yes, certainly You did, Lord. But how does that help me solve *our* suffering?"
>
> "You do not seem to understand the intent of My question. Did I raise Jesus from the dead?"
>
> "Yes. But does it have to happen like this, to someone so young? Why *us*?"
>
> "I repeat My question: Did I raise Jesus from the dead?"
>
> "Sure, but..."
>
> "Then since you know that this is a world where I raised Jesus, would you also say that His teachings are true?"
>
> "Yes, I have always thought that would follow as the best explanation."
>
> "So do you have good reasons for thinking that I am still in control of the universe?"

[2] Gary R. Habermas, "The Truth—and the Comfort—of the Resurrection," *Decision* v. 41, no. 4 (April 2000): 9.

"Yes...You are, Sir. I have no good reason to question that."

"Then is it also the case that, although you do not know why your family is suffering, I do?"

"Well, certainly, I suppose that is true."

"Do you know that, in spite of your suffering, I have chosen you and Debbie in My Son? You will be with Me in heaven for eternity. I promise, you will see her again."

"Lord, I could not even imagine a more glorious truth."

"Does it not follow from the truth of the resurrection?"

"Yes, it would seem to do so..."

"Then what remains? Since you know these things, do you think you can also trust Me in those areas where you do not know all of the answers?"

(Silence)

"I repeat. Do you presently have enough information to trust Me through circumstances that you do not understand?"

"I think you made your points well, my Lord. You got me. I should be trusting You with all my heart."

"Then review these truths often. And do not forget to practice them. Refuse to get sidetracked by other topics, no matter how painful they may seem. Stop carrying your heavy burden by trying to figure everything out. Trust Me with all of your heart."
(emphasis in original)[3]

While this conversation is hypothetical, it illustrates the centrality of the Resurrection to Christian doctrine and everyday life. God sent His Son to earth to save us from our sin. This required the sinless Son of God to be sacrificed on the Cross. But Jesus was vindicated when God raised Him from the dead.

[3] Gary R. Habermas, *The Risen Jesus & Future Hope* (Lanham, MD: Rowman & Littlefield Publishers, Inc., 2003), pp. 192–193.

Our Sympathetic High Priest

One of the great truths of the Incarnation (Jesus coming in the flesh) was explained by the writer of Hebrews:

> Seeing then that we have a great High Priest who has passed through the heavens, Jesus the Son of God, let us hold fast our confession. For we do not have a High Priest who cannot sympathize with our weaknesses, but was in all appoints tempted as we are, yet without sin. Let us therefore come boldly to the throne of grace, that we may obtain mercy and find grace to help in time of need. (Hebrews 4:14-16)

Simply put, Jesus has been in our shoes. He knows what it is like to suffer pain—He suffered far worse than we could ever imagine. He knows what it is like to suffer the loss of a loved one—He "groaned in the spirit and was troubled" and even wept when He witnessed the mourning over Lazarus (John 11:33-35). He knows what it is like to be betrayed by a friend—Judas, one of His disciples, betrayed Him with a kiss (Luke 22:47-48). He knows what it is like to be "deeply distressed" about upcoming events—He was exceedingly sorrowful (Matthew 26:37-38) and even His sweat was like great drops of blood (Luke 22:44). He was falsely accused, mocked, slandered, beaten, denied by friends, and executed even though He was completely innocent.

Our great High Priest, Jesus Christ, has been there before. No matter how difficult life becomes, He's already walked that path, and He can sympathize with us. Because He has been raised from the dead and is now at the right hand of God, we have the liberty to boldly come before "the throne of grace [so] that we may obtain mercy and find grace to help in time of need" (Hebrews 4:16). In fact, He invited people to seek His help:

> Come to Me, all you who labor and are heavy laden, and I will give you rest. Take My yoke upon you and learn from Me, for I am gentle and lowly in heart, and you will find rest for your souls. For My yoke is easy and My burden is light. (Matthew 11:28-30)

Mourning with Hope

Finally, the Resurrection of Jesus can be a tremendous source
of comfort for those who have lost loved ones. Paul told the
Thessalonian believers that the mourning of believers is different
than the unbeliever.

> But I do not want you to be ignorant, brethren,
> concerning those who have fallen asleep, lest you sorrow
> as others who have no hope. For *if we believe that Jesus
> died and rose again*, even so God will bring with Him
> those who sleep in Jesus.
>
> For this we say to you by the word of the Lord, that
> we who are alive and remain until the coming of the Lord
> will by no means precede those who are asleep. For the
> Lord Himself will descend from heaven with a shout,
> with the voice of an archangel, and with the trumpet of
> God. And the dead in Christ will rise first. Then we who
> are alive and remain shall be caught up together with
> them in the clouds to meet the Lord in the air. And thus
> we shall always be with the Lord. Therefore *comfort
> one another with these words*. (1 Thessalonians 4:13–18,
> emphasis added)

One of the great truths of the Resurrection of Jesus is that it not
only made provision for eternal life with God; the Resurrection
also guarantees our future resurrection and gives us "a living
hope" in the present (1 Peter 1:3). We do not mourn like those
who have no hope because we know we will see departed
believing loved ones again. We may miss them terribly, but
someday all believers will be take part in a reunion that will last
for eternity. There will be no more sorrow, pain, grief, tears, and
no more Curse (Revelation 21:3–5, 22:3).

At long last, that great enemy known as death, which entered
our world through the sin of our first parents, will be destroyed
by the risen Savior who conquered the grave (1 Corinthians 15:26).
The Resurrection of Jesus guarantees these glorious truths.
Someday He will return to set things right in this world.

Conclusion

While these truths are comforting for all believers, they should generate great urgency within us to reach the lost with the gospel message. For those who continue to reject Jesus, the Resurrection also guarantees their eternal destruction. Eventually, all people will bow the knee before the Savior who died and rose again, and all will confess, "Jesus Christ is Lord" (Philippians 2:10–11).

If you still have not surrendered your life to the death-conquering Son of God, please continue to read His Word and ask Him to help you understand the truth. Nothing is more important in this world than making sure you are in a right standing with your Creator and Judge. I know of no better way than to end this book on the Resurrection than by restating a couple of passages from the Bible.

> That if you confess with your mouth the Lord Jesus and believe in your heart that God has raised Him from the dead, you will be saved. (Romans 10:9)

> Jesus said to her, "I am the resurrection and the life. He who believes in Me, though he may die, he shall live. And whoever lives and believes in Me shall never die. Do you believe this?" (John 11:25–26)

About the Author

Tim Chaffey is the founder of Midwest Apologetics and is the Content Manager for the Attractions Division of Answers in Genesis. He has earned advanced degrees in Theology, Apologetics, and Church History.

He has authored a dozen books, including *The Truth Chronicles*, a six-volume action-adventure series designed to teach young people to defend the Christian faith and witness to their friends. His popular work, *The Sons of God and the Nephilim*, is his Th.M. thesis with additional content.

Tim is also a leukemia survivor, and his book, *God and Cancer*, uses his battle with blood cancer to discuss the biblical answer to the problem of death and suffering. The book also demonstrates that believers can have hope in life's toughest trials because of who God is and what He's done for us.

A busy writer, Tim maintains a well-trafficked blog at www.midwestapologetics.org/blog and has written numerous magazine and journal articles, as well as hundreds of articles for the Answers in Genesis website. He is a popular speaker on issues related to creation/evolution, dinosaurs, biblical inerrancy, and the Resurrection.

Tim and his wife Casey have two children, Kayla and Judah. In addition to spending time with his family, he enjoys good theological discussions, walking, basketball, swimming, and triathlons.

His books and other resources are available at www.midwestapologetics.org/shop.

CPSIA information can be obtained
at www.ICGtesting.com
Printed in the USA
FFOW05n1706290316